THE URGENT NOW

SERMONS ON CONTEMPORARY
ISSUES
JAMES ARMSTRONG

ABINGDON PRESS

Nashville and New York

THE URGENT NOW

ISBN 0-687-43108-5

Library of Congress Catalog Card Number: 75-109671

Scripture quotations unless otherwise noted are from the Revised Standard Version
of the Bible, copyrighted 1946 and 1952 by the Division of Christian Education,
National Council of Churches, and are used by permission.

Scripture quotations noted Phillips are from *The New Testament in Modern
English,* copyright 1958 by J. B. Phillips.

Scripture quotations noted Goodspeed are from *The Complete Bible, An American
Translation,* by J. M. Powis Smith and Edgar J. Goodspeed, copyright 1939 by the
University of Chicago Press.

Scripture quotations noted TEV are from *Today's English Version of the New
Testament,* copyright 1966 by American Bible Society.

Scripture quotations noted NEB are from the New English Bible, New Testament.
© the Delegates of the Oxford University Press and the Syndics of the Cambridge
University Press 1961. Reprinted by permission.

The lines by Kenneth Boulding on p. 100 are from *There Is a Spirit,* © 1945 by
Fellowship Publications.

The lines of poetry on page 30 are from *Markings* by Dag Hammarskjold. © Copyright 1964 by Alfred A. Knopf, Inc. and Faber & Faber, Ltd. Reprinted by permission
of Alfred A. Knopf, Inc.

The prayer on p. 144 is from "Teach Us the Path, Show Us the Way," from *Are
You Running with Me, Jesus,* by Malcolm Boyd. Copyright © 1965 by Malcolm Boyd.
Reprinted with permission of Holt, Rinehart and Winston, Inc.

The lines by Trinh-Cong-Son on p. 89 are from "The Anguish of the Vietnamese
Artist-Intellectual," by Nam Giang, *Fellowship* (July 1969), p. 16.

SET UP, PRINTED, AND BOUND BY THE
PARTHENON PRESS, AT NASHVILLE,
TENNESSEE, UNITED STATES OF AMERICA

TO
young and old alike who are
asking honest, searching questions
about the place of the Church
in today's world

CONTENTS

"Relevance," "hypocrisy," "freedom," "love," "alienation," "get with it," "where the action is"—these are some of the phrases one hears wherever young people or youthful ideas are involved in today's world. Perhaps a contempt for hypocrisy and a hunger for relevance are two of the more dominant themes of our youth culture. If so, Bishop James Armstrong speaks with rare insight to the youth of America. But he does more than that: he proclaims in the highest traditions of great preaching the enduring claims of love over hate, the spirit of man over the crush of materialism and technology, the imperatives of brotherhood over the folly of war. Anchored by a rich sense of history and a highly informed understanding of the Christian faith, he lives, feels, preaches, and *acts* as a relevant man for today and tomorrow. Bishop Armstrong is at once preacher, philosopher, poet, prophet, and political activist.

It is no longer feasible—if indeed it ever was—to separate one's personal faith from his social responsibility. No true Christian is deserving of peace of soul who does not address himself to the hard issues of war and peace, Vietnam, the arms race, and international community. No Christian worthy of the name can feed his own soul without concern for those around him who hunger in body and spirit. No Christian can really commune with his Creator, who denies the dignity of his fellow creatures by reason of race or class or creed.

More particularly, it is not possible to separate

9

the concerns of religion from the concerns of politics. A religion that is indifferent to the quality of political leadership in society is a religion of doubtful vitality and meaning. Conversely, a political leadership indifferent to the moral claims and insights of religion is a sterile and dangerous leadership. There is no major moral issue now confronting the church which can be fully challenged without involving our political process. But neither is there any major issue in the field of politics that can be adequately challenged without those special insights born of religious and moral convictions.

It is a healthy realism and a commendable humility which prompt Bishop Armstrong to observe that "our churches are often strangely out of step, and usually straggle behind courts and corporations, schools and shows, and even sports contests" in the "drama of life." The church "does not combine the message and the deed. It does not deal with real people and real issues." And again: "Who really cares about apostolic succession or the power of a bishop in Ipswich when people are starving in Biafra, senselessly slaughtered in Vietnam, and crowded into hopeless corners of hate-filled congestion in American ghettos."

But Bishop Armstrong also sees new forces of vitality and relevance moving in today's church—"a new mood abroad . . . impatience with outmoded forms and irrelevant answers . . . a determination to be the church; not a cozy nineteenth-century institution, but a New Testament Church preparing for witness and mission in the twenty-first century."

For working politicians and politically active citizens, the Bishop's chapter "The Christian as Politician" speaks with special force. It is the testament of a man who loves

10

his country deeply enough to call her to a higher standard than the cruel and futile course we have stumbled into in Vietnam. Asserting at once the moral imperatives of his faith and acting effectively to give force to those imperatives by political action, Bishop Armstrong relates his own special effort in the landmark political crucible of 1968. One senses that the author of these lively sermons will continue to make his conscience and his voice meaningful instruments in the battles that lie ahead. International anarchy, national arrogance, nuclear weaponry, technological revolution, the ghetto, poverty, racial explosiveness, human hopelessness—these are the concerns of Bishop Armstrong as preacher and political activist.

The thoughtful reader of these sermons will profit both in the enrichment of his spirit and in new awareness of the urgent claims of the community upon his conscience and his will to action.

George McGovern

For some time critics of preaching have insisted that the sermon has little future and no worthy function in the emerging church. It is, they charge, an outdated form of ministry. Their cynicism seemed confirmed late in 1969, when *The Pulpit,* the prestigious "journal of contemporary preaching," was put to rest after forty years of distinguished service. It has been replaced by a magazine that states: "The mission of the Church requires a new style with new skills for its fulfillment." [1] Does this mean the pulpit is on its way out; that preaching is "old style"? Searching questions are being asked about the place and form of the sermon in the community of faith.

Traditionally, proclamation has been a central function of the church. Even now, few would call for its abandonment. But its role is being reviewed. In his swan song the editor of *The Pulpit* wrote, "We do not intend to minimize preaching; we intend to give this indispensable and demanding task its proper setting by seeing it in relation to the total task of the church's mission." [2] No longer can preaching be seen as an end in itself. It must be viewed against the backdrop of the church's total ministry.

A few months ago I was asked to preach the ordination sermon of one of my former students, a young man who now directs the urban ministries of the Disciples of Christ in greater Los Angeles. The service was held in the United Christian Church of Watts. It was unforgettable. Most of the people there were black. Not too far away was Charcoal Alley, scene of the bloody 1965 riots. The procession that night was led by two Negro girls wearing African dress and carrying crosses. Their hair was "natural"; their bearing, proud. The music—a far cry from Bach—was provided by a folk-and-rock combo called Kind. The congregational "hymns" were, "Blowin' in the Wind," "Let's Get Together," and "He Was a Friend of Mine" (an ode bemoaning the deaths of President Kennedy and Martin Luther King). Representatives of many denominations and secular agencies (the new ecumenicity will be far more than ecclesiastical) were present and participating. I was an outsider, but I joined in the "laying on of hands." After the benediction the combo picked up the beat, a miniskirted vocalist began to sing, and some of the more demonstrative youngsters danced around the chancel.

I had preached—about conflict and reconciliation, community action, national priorities and world peace; about a living Christ at work in today's world. When it was over, a young fellow in a leather jacket came up to me and said my words had *soul*. I hope so. But more important, in that context the sermon was part of a total experience, an experience reaching out beyond the walls and creeds of an institution into the lives and struggles of people.

Preaching today must express and verbalize Christianity's oneness with cultural as well as sacred liturgical forms. It must be linked with social action, community outreach, and a wholistic response to human need. It should be delivered from the trivia, the tired jargon and pedestrian clichés of an earlier era. Rowan and Martin, pop art, and the Woodstock Folk Festival seem far removed from old First Church, but unless the pulpit is aware of their implications it will fail to communicate with the vital masses now shaping tomorrow's world.

In the eye of the pulpit the individual will stand center stage. The sermon will speak to the confused depths of his consciousness. It will affirm a gospel of sensitivity, compassion, and forgiveness. It will try to reinforce the frightened and cheer the lonely and defeated. But even here it dare not provide escape hatches from reality. Our Lord called his hearers to other-centered involvement rather than continual navel-gazing. He challenged his surroundings to embrace life; not to run away from it, to deny or repress it. Stephen Rose calls this eager response to humanity "the way of abandonment" and argues that there will be no renewal of the church apart from it.³ He is right!

Our preaching needs to be balanced. The Christian calendar, with its celebration of Advent and Pentecost, its reflective and passionate remembrance of Lent, its awareness of God's movement in history, should guide thought and preparation. The lectionary, and even an occasional glance at Andrew Blackwood's mechanical "church year," may help us avoid narrow topical phobias. Those who insist that our preaching should be biblical, doctrinal, evangelistic, and devotional are quite correct in their emphasis. But so was the late Bishop Pike when he wrote, "The kerygmatic message in the New Testament gives us what the message is, but does not tell us how to preach it." ⁴ If we cling to thought-forms and verbal landscapes that belong to another day we will lose access to the bright intolerance and secular impatience of the "now generation."

A young man writes about his decision to enter the ministry. He has already earned a master's degree in political science, and has planned a diplomatic career. But after a stint in the Army he has come to feel that his idealism can best be expressed through the church. He writes: "Whatever its failures . . . it still essentially has the answers for which contemporary man is groping. . . . Today's generation has drawn away from the Church because it has proved ineffectual in speaking to current problems and frustrations. This must be rectified."

But how can it be rectified? How can the church speak effectively to current problems and frustrations? (It will take much more than holy talk!)

1. *Through its life-style.* Will the church be more concerned with physical properties and numerical strength than with the drama of life unfolding around it? Will it continue its ostentatious ways, seeking to satisfy its stained-glass, air-conditioned taste buds while much of the world goes hungry, or will it demonstrate selflessness and servanthood?

2. *With an uncompromising approach to mission.* "Mission" is not a gospel word to be sentimentalized; it is an urgent task to be shared. We are called to fields (and congested cities) that are white (and black) unto harvest. In today's world God's people will not seek refuge in customs and buildings that provide security. They will move out into untested areas to grapple with unresolved problems. They will run risks, make mistakes, offend "good" people, and challenge vested interests. Dostoevsky's society woman said, "Love in action is a harsh and dreadful thing compared to love in dreams." Knowing this, God's people will draw strength and inspiration from a cross that was thrown against the sky because of the stubborn courage of their Lord.

3. *With a bold new sense of community.* Self-

conscious barriers between laymen and clergymen, pietists and secularists, grass-roots churches and institutional structures must be erased. While helpful forms of monologue continue, dialogue will be stressed, and the give-and-take of creative conflict will be encouraged rather than denied. Homogenous, "inverted" congregations will give way to colonies of seekers who find their unity not in vapid conformity, but in the freedom of Christ's spirit. While it is true that Stokely Carmichael and George Wallace are members of the same denomination, it is ridiculous to suggest that they are organic members of the same "body"—suffering and rejoicing *together*. Simon the Zealot (a revolutionary pledged to the overthrow of Rome) and Levi (a civil servant employed by Rome) were *one* in their obedient faithfulness. Their political allegiances became secondary as they shared their Lord's ministries. They traveled the countryside, praying, teaching, witnessing, sacrificing, and serving with Jesus, and thus became integral parts of the Twelve—the original community of faith. They didn't talk about *koinonia,* they demonstrated it.

In the light of the above, preaching is not seen as a verbal exercise in a vacuum. It is called to reinforce responsible approaches to the development of Christian life-style, mission, and community. Preaching must also contribute to their realization.

4. If the failures of the past are to be rectified, *there will be the faithful and meaningful proclamation of the Word.* If the pulpit is to play a vital role in the renewal of the church it must be faithful to its biblical roots and rich heritage. But words must be comprehended and applied. They must communicate *meaning.* Perhaps this is what my seminary professor meant when he said every sermon

should contain both the "timeless" and the "timely." If our preaching seeks only to be faithful and true, with little attention given the contemporary scene, it will be neither faithful nor true. Jesus came preaching—to his day—using thought-forms and making references that snagged the minds of his hearers. We are called to do the same. Lilies of the field were a part of his world; pollution is a part of ours. He called scribes and Pharisees into question; we must cope with their bureaucratic counterparts. He talked about swords and Caesar; we talk about nuclear weaponry and Washington. And if, today, we fail to communicate the gospel *in context,* preaching becomes as irrelevant as its critics argue.

The sermons that follow in this slender volume do not present a balanced diet (though I trust there is essential "balance" in each of them). They do not violate the doctrinal or biblical foundations of the faith, but neither do they reflect a self-conscious display of biblical theology. These messages are preoccupied with the here and now. So too are we.

It is my firm conviction that unless the pulpit responds to the major themes and issues of contemporary life it will be deservedly ignored. This must not be permitted. The following then is a modest attempt to offer words of Christian insight and affirmation to this moment of time. It is my prayer you will find them useful.

James Armstrong

Aberdeen, South Dakota

18

At the beginning God expressed himself. That personal expression, that word, was with God and was God, and he existed with God from the beginning. All creation took place through him, and none took place without him. In him appeared life and this life was the light of mankind. . . .
The word of God became a human being and lived among us . . . full of grace and truth.

John 1:1-5, 14 (Phillips)

In the past God spoke to our ancestors many times and in many ways through the prophets, but in these last days he has spoken to us through his Son. He is the one through whom God created the universe, the one whom God has chosen to possess all things at the end. He shines with the brightness of God's glory; he is the exact likeness of God's own being, and sustains the universe with his powerful word. After he had made men clean from their sins, he sat down in heaven at the right side of God, the Supreme Power.

Hebrews 1:1-3 (TEV)

The perfect man is not a myth; he has existed, in the person of Jesus.

Lecomte du Nouy

HOW "MOD" IS CHRIST?

Our recent national history has been a story of extremes. Assassins' bullets have claimed the lives of John F. Kennedy, Martin Luther King, and Robert Kennedy. Indescribable poverty and hunger have been uncovered on our very doorstep. Students continue to make their demands and burn their draft cards. The Negro has brushed aside the sacred barricades and entered the church with his Black Manifesto. We still engage in pious double-talk as Vietnam is being destroyed.

But the other side of the ledger is impressive too. Our national prosperity continues unchecked. There was less violence in our cities last summer than the summer before. Schools are being desegregated across the southland (although the process seems far more political than humane). And we did land those men on the moon, didn't we? History has never known a moment quite like this. Yet the melodrama of America's recent past gives us but a glimpse of the world in microcosm.

We have our astronauts; but Russia has her cosmonauts and Red China detonates her H-bombs.

Our political heroes die; but so does Ho Chi Minh, and Tom Mboya is shot down in Africa.

We have our social unrest; but so do Czechoslovakia, Greece, Brazil, and Libya. And the Middle East threatens to blow itself off the map.

Student revolt is not limited to the American campus; the student generation has challenged an assortment of Establishments in Rome, Paris, West Berlin, Mexico City, and Tokyo.

Hunger is not confined to Mississippi's Delta and to Collier County in Florida. There is mass starvation in Biafra.

God only knows what this year will bring—and next. "It's a new ball game." Cybernetics, technology, radical changes in transportation and communication, and a wild assortment of revolutions have seen to that. It is a frightening, awe-inspiring, utterly unprecedented moment of time. Science fiction has become present fact. Tomorrow we may all be playing hide-and-seek among the stars, if we don't first blast ourselves into oblivion. In such a world, at such a time, we seek to be Christian. Strange aspiration! We sing the same old songs, pray the same old prayers, use the same old words and phrases, as if things could ever be the same again. Where does the church fit into a world like this? Where do Christians fit into such a world? And what about our Lord Christ? How "mod" is he? Does he have any meaning for all this?

If we are honest we will confess that the images Christ brings to mind are often timeworn and irrelevent.

For instance, there is the *Jesus of childhood memory.* I remember. I remember a country church with papered-over windows; the musty smell of the church basement; a dear old Sunday school teacher with paste in one hand and Bible in the other; and the upright piano banging out the jubilant tunes; "Bringing in the Sheaves," "Onward, Christian Soldiers," and "Church in the Wildwood."

And there were those hero stories. There was Joseph and his psychedelic robe; Samson and his hair; Delilah and her shears; David and his slingshot; Goliath and his size. To a little boy, Jesus just didn't measure up in that company. He hadn't killed any giants or pulled a temple down with his bare hands. We sang the sentimental words:

> Jesus, the very thought of thee
> With sweetness fills my breast;
> But sweeter far thy face to see,
> And in thy presence rest.

I don't care if Bernard of Clairvaux did write those lines, what did they mean to a youngster nurtured on the legends of Robin Hood and the exploits of Dick Tracy? And how can that kind of a Jesus be related to jungle warfare in Vietnam and the hopelessness of ghetto living? Does the Jesus of childhood memory speak to the plight of contemporary man?

More to the point, *what about the Christ of creedal statement?* The diet of my early years was much the same as yours. It included the Pledge of Allegiance, the Lord's Prayer, "My Country, 'Tis of Thee," and almost every Sunday, the Apostles' Creed (with the words not given a second thought). Week after week I repeated them: "I believe in God the Father Almighty, . . . and in Jesus Christ his only Son our Lord." The Creed is a majestic statement of faith, but it was framed in a day that expressed itself in far different ways than we do. Not only that, but it skips the life of Jesus. It leaps from "born of the Virgin Mary" to "suffered under Pontius Pilate" with hardly a pause for a comma.

The creeds of the church, valuable as they are as teaching instruments and reflections of history, do not reveal a *living* Christ. Don't misunderstand. Creeds have their place. In a sense they are custodians of the past. They probe the hidden meanings of eternal truth. But they should be seen as guideposts, not straitjackets.

We need to remind ourselves of the obvious at this point. Both the Jesus of childhood memory and the Christ of ancient creed emerge from the pages of sacred scripture. In the introductory words of John's Gospel and the letter to the Hebrews we see man being prepared by God for His climactic self-expression. More than a hundred years ago Robertson of Brighton said it like this: "God had a Word to spell: His own name. Letter by letter, syllable by syllable he wrote until at last it came entire. The Word was made flesh and dwelt among us."

All right, but how is this to be communicated to the present age? *What is the significance of the Christ-event for our time?* We dwell in a new kind of world.

Atomic bombs are not just bigger bombs.

Electronic computers are not just bigger adding machines.

Megapolis is not just a bigger city.

Neil Armstrong's space flight to the moon was not just the story of Columbus or the Wright Brothers retold.

These are manifestations of a "new order." When the Christian says that his Lord came "not to condemn the world, but to save it," he is talking about *this* world— about *these* worlds—the worlds of Cape Kennedy and urban sprawl, of nuclear warheads and biochemical weaponry, of population explosion and indescribable poverty and hunger. And if Christ cannot save these worlds, then he is not the promised Savior of *the world*, period!

Let's be clear about this. Christ transcends the here and now. He is not limited to this moment of time or this spot of earth. When Bruce Barton turned Jesus into a public relations expert and supersalesman in *The Man Nobody Knows*, he missed the point entirely. So does "Broadway Joe" Namath when he justifies his beard by reminding us that Jesus wore one. Christ was not a bright young man in a grey flannel suit nor a pontifical holy man, any more than he was a mod, cool, groovy flower child. He cannot be neatly deposited in the pocket of any particular culture, however valid that culture may be. Christ is Christ, *the* Christ, the unique Son and revelation of the living God. Michael Harrington, the ideological "father" of America's war on poverty, said an essential word when he wrote:

The Church will not regain its vitality . . . by simply being hipper than thou. It must, to be sure, fight for the earthly implications of the heavenly values it affirms; it can never again divorce God from the Negroes, the poor, those dying in war and the rest of humanity. *But over and above that witness . . . there must be the assertion of the eternal.*

If there is to be, in fact, "a new Church for a new world," that Church will find its authority and power in faithful obedience to an eternal, now-living Christ!

"In the beginning was the Word, and the Word was with God, and the Word was God." (John 1:1.)

"It was little by little and in different ways [through nature, history, poet, priest, and prophet] that God spoke in old times . . . but in these latter days he has spoken to us in a Son." (Heb. 1:1-2 Goodspeed.)

The Christ of the eternal ages is our present hope. He is our contemporary. As Louis Cassels points out in his fine book *The Real Jesus,* Christ was no gentle Jesus, meek and mild. "He was a bold, outspoken man who rebelled against convention and trampled unmercifully on the tenderest corns of the religious and political establishment." [1]

If we are to have a new church it must be faithful to the Christ who broke with his past and promised to "make all things new."

Christ turned to the hated Samaritan and dared to *love.*

He turned to the wretched woman of the streets and *accepted* her; *forgave* her; restored her *hope* and *self-respect.*

He turned to the unwashed and rejected, and *became one with them.*

He sought out the winebibber and glutton, the publican and sinner, and said, *"I'm yours!* The Son of man has come to seek and to save *the lost!"*

He brought with him no mood of harsh retaliation; no fierce, impersonal sense of judgment. Rather, he came to preach to the poor, heal the broken, and deliver the captive.

The church exists not to protect us from harsh reality, not to spare us from confronting the unpleasant problems of our day. It is here to *involve* us. If we are "in Christ" we will join him in his redemptive work in our frightening world.

Sometime ago a cartoon appeared in the *New Yorker* magazine. Two couples were playing bridge; obviously they had been talking about the race problem. One of the wives, addressing her husband, said, "Henry, your train runs through Harlem every day. What do you think?" That is how too many of us approach the contemporary scene. We whiz past the Indian reservation and the farm-workers' shacks on the superhighway, race through the ghetto on the subway, listen to locker-room conversation at the club, read William Buckley and David Lawrence, turn off David Brinkley, and draw our firm conclusions. We are not involved! Surrounded by people who look, talk, act, and think exactly as we do, we simply reflect our limited surroundings. From such an isolated vantage point we make up our minds on the most crucial issues of the day. Such a posture, though understandable, cannot be justified for the *Christian* in our kind of world.

Following the murder of Martin Luther King, the city-wide memorial service in Indianapolis was held in the church I was then privileged to serve. More than 2,000 people were there, half-black, half-white. The mayor of the city spoke, as did civil rights and religious leaders. The massed choir sang, "The Battle Hymn of the Republic." Soul music was sung. A young black seminarian had memorized notable passages from the writings of Dr. King. With deep feeling he quoted them. At last we all joined hands and sang, "We Shall Overcome." The entire service was broadcast. A few moments after it went off the air the radio station received a telephone call from a young man who identified himself as a black militant. His voice was trembling as he said, "I've just heard all those people there together, and I've been wrong. I've hated 'Whitey' and wanted the war to break out between us, but maybe there's hope. What can I do?" God was in Christ—working through his church in that moment—reconciling.

I know there are no simple, overnight answers to the confused problems of the day. Education has its place, and we must honor it. Enlightened legislation has its place, and we must encourage it. The courts have their place, and we must support them. Humanitarian concern has its place, and we must be a part of that concern. But the Christian has a unique word to say:

I slept. I dreamed. I seemed to
climb a hard, ascending track
And just behind me labored one
whose face was black.
I pitied him, but hour by hour he
gained upon my path.
He stood beside me, stood upright, and
then I turned in wrath.
"Go back," I cried, "what right have
you to stand beside me here?"
I paused, struck dumb with fear,
for low! The black man was not there—
But Christ stood in his place!
And oh! the pain, the pain, the pain
that looked from that dear face.[2]

Don't you see? We are called to find the Christ in every man; to respond to the Christ in every man; and to join the Christ in his ministry to every situation. Christ can be limited by our limitations and silenced by our silence. Or we can move with him into his world, proclaim his reality in unexpected places, and seek to extend the Incarnation into this year of our Lord.

27

Do you remember Runty Nolan in Budd Schulberg's *Waterfront?* There had been trouble on the docks. A corrupt labor union imported strong-arm hoodlums, and they killed Nolan. His body was recovered from the Hudson River, and Father Barry was summoned to the waterfront to pronounce the last rites. But Father Barry didn't stop there. After administering the sacrament he angrily glared at the dock workers and said: "You want to know what's wrong with our waterfront? . . . It's love of a lousy buck. . . . The fat profit—the wholesale stealing—the cushy job—more important than the love of man. It's forgetting that every fellow down here is your brother, yes, your brother in Christ."

The author continued:

The word *Christ* wasn't spread over them softly as a balm. It was hurled at them as a gauntlet, as a furious challenge. . . . For them it was a hell of a shock to be urged to make room for a living Christ who stood among them in a windbreaker, carrying a cargo hook in His hand, a Christ Who wondered how He was going to meet His rent and His grocery bill, a Christ crucified by loan sharks and strong-armers, a Christ on a North River cross, dumped like garbage or Runty Nolan, tied up with bailing wire, into the muck of the Hudson.[3]

We dare not confine Christ to sentimental childhood memory. He cannot be entombed in creed or hymn or stained-glass window. He will not be kept under wraps, in flowing black robes or within four cozy walls. *He is alive! His Spirit is at work in our world!* Our task is to find him *out there*—to become one with him *out there;* to enter into his suffering and his pain for a waylost humanity; to take up the towel of servanthood and the mandate of the cross, that men might live as brothers and "justice roll down like waters, and righteousness like a mighty stream."

The eternal Christ is Lord of this moment of time. We are called to find him here, to experience and proclaim his *present* reality, and to extend his will and spirit into the harsh realities of the here and now.

CHAPTER 2

*I am being driven forward
Into an unknown land.
The pass grows steeper,
The air colder and sharper.
A wind from my unknown goal
Stirs the strings
Of expectation*
Dag Hammarskjold

*The wind blows where it wills; you hear the sound of
it, but you do not know where it comes from, or where
it is going. So with everyone who is born from spirit.*
John 3:8 (NEB)

THE WHEREABOUTS OF GOD...

Where is God in such a world? In us? In folk like us? In empty souls and shattered nerves and senses driven wild by film and ad and constant titillation?

Where is God in such a world? On streets of fear, where muggers lurk and rapists ply their trade? Where pickets march and scholars plead, and generations are separated by so much more than years?

Where is God in such a world? In Birmingham, where police dogs strain against the leash, and snarl, and bare their teeth at trembling old ladies painted black by nature's brush?

Where is God in such a world? In sniper's nest? In homemade bomb? In the mad shriek "Burn, baby, burn," as cities turn to ashes overnight?

Where is God in such a world? In rocket and napalm?

This sermon was first preached at Riverside Church in New York City. Later, in an abbreviated form, it was heard on NBC's "Art of Living." This accounts for the letter from a listener that follows the sermon.

In earth that's scorched? In a village peasant's scream and a dying soldier's whimpering cry?

Where is God in such a world? Where is God?

Bob Dylan, occasional folk singer and conscience of the American young, strums his guitar and asks how many deaths it will take till we know that too many people have died. He goes on:

> The answer . . . is blowin' in the wind;
> The answer is blowin' in the wind.[1]

"The wind blows where it wills; you hear the sound of it, but you don't know where it comes from or where it is going. . . ." Where is God in such a world? Like the wind he is free Spirit, not confined, not contained, but moving in and through all things. No longer is it enough to rely upon the familiar clichés and dogmas of the past. We can philosophize, theologize, and traditionalize all we choose. But there come times when, with backs against the wall and minds confused, we find little comfort in the bold doctrines of the past. We hunger for present reality. We listen to the arguments, brush them aside, and cry, "Yes, but where is *God* in all this?"

Let's begin where we are. *God is here with us, in this world.* Not "up" there, or "out" there, but *here,* in the unraveling events of our time. God does not coerce history. He is not John Calvin's God, playing the puppeteer as he determines the acts and directions of our lives. He does not force events to happen. But he does inspire some of them, judge all of them, and share in their consequences with each of us.

This is no new theology. It is as old as man's search for truth. It is at the heart of the biblical revelation. The God of Moses was the God of current events. At no time did Moses attempt to reduce God to a definition. Systems of thought and abstract terms were foreign to him. "I am that I am," said Moses' God. God *is!* He *exists!* He *functions,* in relationship and behavior.

Moses' God is the God of covenant, who binds man to man not only in primitive tribal community, but in an emerging urban society.

He is the God of law—of ethics—who reveals the requisites of the good life not only from an Arabian mountaintop 3,500 years ago, but also to all men in every age in the deeps of their own beings.

He is the God who works through people. By locking Moses up in a religious showcase, we have lost sight of the humanity, the audacity, and the far-reaching influence of the man. Moses was a flesh-and-blood mortal used by God to redirect the course of human history.

We mutter about preachers who dabble in politics. We complain about religious cranks and zealots who march and protest and become involved in controversy. Look at Moses! That was no doddering old bishop he confronted. That was the mightiest ruler of his time. And Moses cried: "You let my people go." When his plea fell on deaf ears, he returned to the victims of his nation's tyranny, identified with them, organized them, marched with them, and led them from their bondage, pursued by troops that served under the flag of his land. That wasn't a church council he was challenging, not a vestry or a synod or an administrative board. That was the Pentagon; that was the White House; that was the Establishment of his day.

We sometimes criticize those who would broaden the base of the community of faith to include the unwashed and the unwanted. Again we find little comfort in Moses.

While he was on a mountaintop his unruly followers got drunk. They built a god of gold. They danced and sang and celebrated. The fact is that when their leader returned to them they were caught up in an orgy that would make Hugh Hefner's Chicago "pad" look like a Salvation Army headquarters. Did Moses read them out of the party? Excommunicate them? Did he reject them? No. He was angry. He threw things. But the following morning he slipped out and prayed. He pled with God to forgive this sinful people. Then he added, "And, God, if you won't do that, then erase my name from your book of life." If irresponsible rebels could not be included in God's community, then Moses chose to be an outsider too.

The God of Moses was a God of people and of life, as was the God of Abram and Isaiah and Job. This "historical theology" comes into even sharper focus in the *new* covenant. It is the meaning of the Incarnation. God became real in an event, the Christ-event. God acted out his nature and his will in history. No intricate arguments passed the lips of the Nazarene. He was not a doctrinaire apologist; not a systematic theologian. He was a *doer* of the truth. Yet because of Jesus we have drawn certain conclusions about God.

God is love, we say. What does that mean? Well, how does love respond to the hated Samaritan (or was he a Puerto Rican?); to the loose, immoral woman (or was she a homosexual?); to the screaming madman (a paranoid husband? a neurotic wife?)? Love is not a concept to be debated; it is acceptance of the rejected. It is an attitude that tries to understand, and a deed that needs to be done.

God is Spirit, we say. What does that mean?

The answer . . . is blowin' in the wind,
The answer is blowin' in the wind.[2]

"God is spirit, and they who worship him must worship him in spirit." Like the wind, spirit comes and goes on its own terms. In Christ, spirit was not codified but exemplified. The Spirit of God is compassion, understanding, forgiveness; it is justice tempered by mercy; it is anguish in the face of grief, indignation in the face of wrong, and joy in the presence of life well-lived. God is spirit. God is love. *God is suffering involvement.* Enter the cross—in history—again, an event at a time and a place. God took upon himself the form of a servant. As Bonhoeffer said, "In Jesus Christ the reality of God entered into the reality of this world."[3] God was in Christ, *reconciling.*

The biblical revelation cares little for metaphysics. Our mechanical devotion to theological exercises and doctrinal disputation fails to grasp that fundamental fact. For the most part, the Bible is concerned with people, events, and historical meanings.

I have mentioned Dietrich Bonhoeffer. The German martyr wrote at length about the "worldliness" of God and the "worldliness" of discipleship. He argued that God is not a religious God preoccupied with "religious" ceremonies, but a God who is passionately involved in the agony of a suffering world. He argued that the supernatural is found in the natural, the holy in the profane, and the revelational in the rational. Thus, the Christian will be at home in seats of commerce and halls of state, with the academician and the precinct committeeman, at the country club and in the darkest, foulest corner of the ghetto. If faithfulness is not related to this *real* world of

35

ours, then who do we think we are kidding—and why bother with the symbols and forms of the gospel?

Immersed in the history of his moment of time, Dietrich Bonhoeffer was a "contemporary Christian." Like Moses, he opposed his Pharaoh, Adolf Hitler. Like Moses, he identified with a community in bondage.

But unlike Moses, Bonhoeffer did not have the option of a distant wilderness. His wilderness was right there, within the boundaries of the Third Reich, denouncing Hitler's lust for power, plotting against Hitler, and at last, being hanged for his "crimes against the state."

It is easy for us to see God in Bonhoeffer's martyrdom. Jews were being slaughtered, and Hitler was trying to take over the world. It is easy for us to see God in the martyrdom of Christians in Red China who have died bearing witness to their faith. We can see God at work in history in distant places and in former years. But what about here—on our own doorstep—in the United Nations, in the peace movement, among black-power advocates, in the relief of poverty and the responsible use of wealth? This is where the rub comes. Faithful discipleship does not require an intellectual appreciation of God's participation in past events. It does require an awareness of his participation in current events, and a sharing with him in the redirection of human affairs here and now.

Does this mean that we will all become marching, shouting, demonstrating activists? Not necessarily, though we will better understand why others do. It does mean, however, that we will see the difference between irrational looting and murder on the one hand, and angry demands for social justice on the other; between sinful treason on the one hand, and draft resistance and war protest on the other. And if we do not recognize these differences, we have not done our homework well and we do not understand the claims of the gospel. God is at work in today's world. God is present wherever man protects freedom with the tools of freedom; wherever regional and parochial idols are smashed because our loyalties transcend this particular spot of earth; wherever responsible peace is pursued; wherever love and justice are structured into social process; wherever the rights of man are protected and his responsibilities assumed; wherever the values of the Christian faith are placed above all other loyalties of life.

If God is dead for some of us, maybe it is because we have barred him from those particular worlds in which we really do our living. By insisting that God has no right to enter into this compartment, or this relationship, or this prior commitment, we deny Him. This is how God is silenced and how he dies.

Long ago Jesus said, "Go ye into all the world." An English churchman, commenting on that phrase, said, "We have made that mean Africa and Fiji and Calcutta, but it means more relevantly the world of computers and biochemistry and politics."[4] God is the God of our world, the world of the here-and-now, or he is no God at all. He is a worldly God, and we are called to a worldly faithfulness and discipline. God comes alive for us as we acknowledge his sovereignty over all things and find him not in faulty definitions and institutions, but in the events of everyday. *In our response to these events we are tried and tested.* God is our judge, and history is his judgment upon us.

AND A LETTER IN RESPONSE

Rev. Armstrong,

You're a beautiful cat, man, really beautiful. Last Saturday night my friends and I got "stoned" and we left the radio on. About 6:30 when some of us started "gettin' straight" we heard you quoting Bob Dylan's "Blowin' in the Wind," and we just couldn't believe it. All of us gathered around the radio and started diggin' every word you were saying. We loved it man, really loved it. We always thought "Blowing in the Wind" was like getting high on grass, but we really dug the way you put it. Some of the girls started crying and some of the guys, sitting cross-legged, nodded their heads up and down and murmured, "yes, yes."

It really tore me up, Rev. Armstrong, I swear I'll never forget it. I looked around at my friends, some of the seventeen and eighteen year olds, some of them in their middle twenties, but all of them seemed "old." Girls with their eyes bugged wide from the "ups," guys with their eyes hazed grey from the "smoke," and some of them stone straight, yet all of them digging what you said. It damn near broke my heart to look at them. I remember eight or nine years ago when I was just starting out as a teen-ager, I remember kids with "hot-rods," drinking beer and laughing at stupid "knock-knock" jokes. But my god, what's happened? Sixteen-year-old girls "shoot-up" for a kick, and by the time they are eighteen they are worn out, used up, too beat to think about the future. Nobody laughs anymore. We're raping the next generation of any hope for a childhood.

I see my friends sit around and talk at a party. No "spin the bottle" or "making out." Elvis Presley and a session in the "back seat" are dead. They worry about their subconscious guilt from their white ancestors and what they can do to help the black man. They talk about the Indian and how noble he was before the "civilized white man" came. They all know the hypocrites we are when Johnson condemns Russia over Czechoslovakia and then signs orders to drop napalm on peasants. They know it all, nobody laughs, and they're old, man, old and tired of it all. They cry when somebody mentions Jack, Bobby or Martin. So we "smoke," pop a pill or do our "own thing," and soon it all goes away like a bad dream.

But as a lost ship at sea must feel when it spies a safe harbor, we heard your broadcast and some of us smiled and some of us cried. But we all dug what you said about "love" and "god as a spirit."

If there really is people like you left in the church, maybe there's hope after all. Maybe.

So I just wanted to say "thanks," "keep the faith, baby" and why the hell don't you get on prime time so the "establishment" can hear your message instead of listening to dog-biscuit commercials!

Stay with it man,

(signature)

The above letter came to me following the NBC broadcast of "The Whereabouts of God." Crude and shocking as it may seem to some, it reflects an unusual level of spiritual hunger and ethical sensitivity. We can ignore voices such as these if we choose—but only by betraying the very ones our Lord loved and died for.

CHAPTER 3

The thing that keeps coming back to me is, what is Christianity, and indeed what is Christ, for us today?

Dietrich Bonhoeffer

Now when Jesus give over talking you could a eard a pin drop. Folks just couldn't get over it. Cos e knew what e was talking about—dey could all see dat. E was as sharp as a razor, as clear as day and as sure of imself as the sun in Eaven. E wasn't like the scribes. There was no hummin and hawin wid Jesus.

Matthew 7:27, 28 (The Gospels in Scouse)

THE "TODAY SHOW"

Sometime ago Ken Jackson and Mel Rivers, ex-convicts, were on NBC's "Today Show." They have forsaken their lives of crime, and are now devoting themselves to crime prevention and the rehabilitation of criminals. They have joined the Fortune Society, a kind of "ex-convicts anonymous." Where did they hear about the Fortune Society? On David Susskind's late-night TV show. And where did the Fortune Society come from? It was inspired by an off-Broadway play. Here were two men who had literally been converted from one way of life to another. Where did the church fit into the process? Nowhere—absolutely nowhere.

You see, the "Today Show"—the contemporary scene—is preempting the church.

Government and private agencies are caring for the physical needs of people. Social protest has been largely taken over by black power, student power, the New Left and "flower children."

Alcoholics Anonymous, the Fortune Society, and groups trying to help homosexuals, potential suicides, and drug addicts have developed their specialized and often highly effective ministries.

Even the entertainment world, long an object of religious scorn, is saying a redeeming word. Hollywood and Broadway are asking basic questions with rare freshness and honesty. How can we better understand the generation gap? Have you seen *The Graduate* or *Goodby, Columbus* or *Easy Rider?* What about the collapse of family life in a bored, well-to-do, empty middle-class society? Did you see *Faces?* What about the pros and cons of law enforcement? Have you seen *Pendulum?* How could you miss the Christ-figure in Paul Newman's *Cool Hand Luke* or the seering indictment of war in *Shame?* Read the scripts of Edward Albee, John Osborne, and Tennessee Williams and you will discover that "sin" is far more than a religious catchword. *Fiddler on the Roof* is a delightful play by almost any standard, but look at it as a wholesome and penetrating study of the so-called new morality. And what about the grandest and most demanding question of all: what is life's meaning? Of course we will search the Scriptures (at least we say we will). We will find guidance in the classics. Viktor Frankl, Rollo May, and other present-day seers will prove helpful. But have you seen Ingmar Bergman's *trilogy?* Have you studied the life and development of this Swedish filmmaker, one of the creative geniuses of our time?

Statisticians tell us that church attendance is down in America. Why? Is it because we are becoming an irreligious people? Is there some plot afoot to destroy the churches? No. It's just that the scene may be changing; the action may be elsewhere. Or to put it another way: the church in mission is moving far beyond the forms and walls of our ecclesiastical institution. The "Today Show" described the transformation of two confirmed criminals because of the impact of the late-night talk show and an off-Broadway play. That's the way things are today!

The drama of life continues to unfold. The fundamental questions are still being asked. But our churches are often strangely out of step and usually straggle behind courts and corporations, schools and shows, and even sports contests. If institutional religion is to regain its authority and authenticity, it must rediscover that passionate commitment to Christ and passionate involvement in his world that are at the heart of the New Testament.

Sometime ago, in response to a statement I had made about capital punishment, I received a letter from an irate church member. The writer took me to task for leaving my field, religion, and meddling in something that was "none of [my] business." He said, "What are we here for? To cure the world's ills or to preach the gospel of salvation?" With him it was an either/or proposition. We are not called to try to heal the world; we are simply commissioned to talk about it.

Well, we are commissioned to talk about it. *The church—your church—exists to proclaim the Gospel.*

Mark wrote, "Jesus came into Galilee, proclaiming the gospel of God." Peter, at Pentecost, proclaimed the living reality of God in Christ. Paul, standing before his king, told of his conversion—his literal turning-about—on the Damascus Road, and then added, "To this very day . . . I stand to testify . . . concerning the death, resurrection, and [universality] of Christ." That is proclamation! He said, "Woe is me, if I preach not the gospel." From then until now, from the bold declaration of the *kerygma* in the primitive church to the colorful drama of Bishop Sheen on ABC, from Chrysostom in Constantinople and Savonarola in Florence to Billy Graham in Madison Square Garden, God has used the "foolishness of preaching."

The proclamation of the gospel is not the bellowing of a town crier who shouts interesting news from the street corner. Proclamation is the breaking of the bread of life; it is a shared covenant between the messenger, the hearer, and God himself. The town crier, the journalist, if you please, can be indifferent to the news he spreads. But the faithful witness speaks from within the Christ-event, is involved in God's present self-revelation, and is inspired and possessed by the divine spirit.

The church of Jesus Christ exists to declare the good news. It should never apologize for talking. Moses spoke and slaves revolted. Isaiah spoke and kings listened. Jeremiah spoke and a nation was called to repentance. Jesus spoke and "the common people heard him gladly," as history changed its course.

Self-styled authorities from Marshall McLuhan to Malcolm Boyd argue that preaching is a thing of the past. Nonsense! Much of the preaching we hear may be dead. But that simply means that the preachers have not done their homework. They haven't studied. They haven't kept abreast of current affairs. They have drifted from the roots of their faith. They have been slipshod in their methods and careless in their disciplines. This is not a reflection on the function of preaching. It is a reflection on preachers—on people like me, who have refused to pay the price.

Don't tell me preaching is dead. The power of the spoken word still sways the minds of men. Adolf Hitler used the power of speech to pervert the will of a nation. Fidel Castro brought a revolution into being with inflamed oratory. George Wallace imposed himself on the

American people—and was the most effective campaigner on the trail in 1968—because he knew how to manipulate fearful people with words. Or look at the other side of the coin. The "Today Show" is a talk show. David Susskind talks with his guests. An off-Broadway play verbalizes ideas. And life is changed. Criminals become reformers. They tell others about it, using the communications media. Why should the church abandon an art that is the backbone of Madison Avenue, the rage of the networks, and a key to political and social change? Augustine understood all this. He once said, "By means of the arts of rhetoric both truth and falsehood are urged. Who would dare say that truth should stand unarmed while those who urge falsehood prevail?"

Jesus came preaching—make no mistake about that! *What* he said and *who* he said it to were important. But more important was the message he spelled out in living deed. He *did* the truth.

In his very first public statement he said he had come to preach to the poor and deliver the captive. If the chronology of Matthew is to be believed, he preached the so-called Sermon on the Mount shortly thereafter. Now the Sermon on the Mount was no calm and soothing preachment. It was a disturbing, perhaps even rabble-rousing, plea to conscience. It praised virtues others scorned. It turned away from the honored religion and binding law of a treasured past and said, "This isn't good enough for us anymore." It praised unselfish love, condemned petty judgment, and internalized morality. It presumed to know the will of God and to declare it. And the people who heard it, because they saw the integrity of his life, said Jesus spoke as one having authority. As *The*

Gospels in Scouse says, "There was no hummin and hawin wid Jesus."

Maybe church attendance is falling off, maybe the church is relatively ineffective today because it is not living the life it proclaims. It hums and haws. *It does not combine the message and the deed. It does not deal with real people and real issues.*

What do we too often hear from the pulpits of the land? Fuzzy abstractions about sin and salvation. Words piled on words about ecclesiastical and behavioral trivia. Gauntlets thrown down and challenges hurled out with no accompanying book of instructions, with no specifics attached; so high moments are dissipated and emotional catharsis becomes a substitute for genuine servanthood. Or the flaming issues of the day are swept under the rug because of cowardice shared. Ideas—profound biblical, theological, and ethical ideas—are treated as ends in themselves, while flesh-and-blood people are somehow lost in the shuffle.

As a husband, I need to see my home not in an impossible, idealized form, but as a very human and demanding constellation of moods, attitudes, and relationships. As a male, I need to better understand my role as father, and my wife's role as mother, and our children. (Even as I seek to guide, discipline, and "free" our children, I must, above all, try to understand them.) I am a professional man. How does my daily work life, my energy invested, relate to the health and hope or to the sickness of today's world? The same question could be asked of the construction foreman, the sales executive, the housewife. I am a citizen. I need to analyze the urgent problems of my time in the light of the faith I profess. I am a man. How am I to understand the depths, the contradictions, and longings of my inner worlds? What does my church say to me about the struggles I really face and the life I really live? Or does it just talk about fellowship suppers and the tribes of Israel and Sunday school attendance goals?

The church needs to deal with real people and with real issues if it is to be a serious factor in today's world. Real issues . . . *real issues*—not the fabrications of little minds. Who really cares about apostolic succession or the power of a bishop in Ipswich when people are starving in Biafra, senselessly slaughtered in Vietnam, and crowded into hopeless corners of hate-filled congestion in American ghettoes.

Colin Morris, former president of the United Church of Zambia, has written a frightful book called *Include Me Out*. It is frightful because, like Kierkegaard's *Attack upon Christendom*, it exposes our damning hypocrisy and presumption. Morris opens his book with these words: "The other day a Zambian dropped dead not a hundred yards from my front door. The pathologist said he'd died of hunger. In his shrunken stomach were a few leaves and what appeared to be a ball of grass, . . . nothing else."[1] Later that same day Dr. Morris received in the mail his copy of the *Methodist Recorder*. Its columns were filled with the white heat of righteous indignation. The final report of the Anglican-Methodist Unity Commission had been postponed. Suddenly Colin Morris saw all of the painfully elaborate machinations of the institutional church through the dead eyes of a little man with a shrunken belly. "Little men with shrunken bellies call the Church's bluff," he wrote.[2]

Do you know that 495 out of every 1,000 people on the face of this earth earn less than $100 a year? That 670 out of every 1,000 people on this planet suffer from malnutrition? That thousands of persons continue to starve in Biafra? Our Lord said he had come to preach to the poor. He taught us to pray for daily bread. He said, "Inasmuch as you have given food to the hungry you have fed me." Eminent scientists are telling us that by 1975 there will be certain widespread famine on the face of the earth. Are we responding to the real issues of existence as our Lord defined them, or simply quibbling over the study books our circles should report on?

And what of war? The leveling of the Mekong Delta city of Ben Tre during the Tet offensive of 1968 was a perfect illustration of war's madness. A thousand communists, we said, had infiltrated a *South* Vietnamese town of 35,000 people. (Now remember: these were our allies, our "comrades in arms.") We brought up our firepower, our 500-pound bombs, napalm, rockets, and our 105 and 155mm artillery, and we let 'em have it. Hundreds, perhaps thousands, of innocent civilians were killed. A colonel from Chicago said, "We'll never know for sure how many. Hundreds of them are buried forever under the rubble." And an Army officer, talking to a newspaper correspondent, said, "In order to save the city we had to destroy it." That single statement epitomizes the insanity of our self-righteous, fire-breathing logic. Who are we to determine by force of arms the destinies of millions of people on the other side of the world?

Now add to the indefensibility of our stance in Vietnam and the utter futility of war itself the stark, the terrifying, fact of the H-bomb, and you begin to see the outlines of a *real issue* confronting the church. A young friend of ours, a college student, writing about the backwash of the bomb, described it this way:

48

Little tree—
Your tortured limbs and yellowed
   leaves are the last signs of life.
Hold me—
Too weak to stand, too crippled
   to lie; tree, support me as
   my last breath passes.
Was it all a dream?
Tell me, bush, did smiling faces,
   noisy streets, quiet parks
   ever exist?
Is nothing as it seems?
Dust and ashes now pile where
   I thought my sister was
   sleeping in the grass.
It's us alone.
Are we alone? Have years of
   work and meaning come to
   this—disintegration?
Lord, make yourself known!
Tree, answer please. Where have
   they put Him; what has
   become of Him?
Where is God? . . .[3]

Jesus said, "Love your enemy. . . . Do good to those who
despitefully use you. . . . Blessed are the peacemakers."
While we are debating the legitimacy of the new forms
and liturgies in our churches, a mushroom cloud gathers
on the far horizon and everything we hold dear teeters at
the abyss of a new Dark Age.

I dare say Hugh Downs was there again this morning
with the "Today Show." The latest news was featured, and
conversations dealt with real people and real issues. What
will we think about at next Sunday morning's worship ser-

vice? Will Bach be played and Fannie Crosby sung? (They do have their place, you know.) Will we talk about infant baptism, the size of a whale's stomach, the dimensions of a temple in Jerusalem, mini-skirts, and occasional martinis? Will we laboriously face questions no one is asking? Really now! These are days of crisis. People are in agony. The church exists for such a time as this.

That disturbing Colin Morris, unable to forget the dead man with the shrunken belly, wrote: "What, after all, is the Church *for?* . . . She exists to report an Event [the Christ-event] by *re-enacting it.*" [4] The Sermon on the Mount dominates the landscape of the New Testament because our Lord lived its message. Our *proclamation* of the gospel will derive its authority from our *demonstration* of the gospel. Unless, through the church, the incarnation is extended into this moment of time; unless, in the presence of the cross, we are willing to give ourselves away; unless, in and through people like us the Christ-event is *reenacted,* the community of faith will have no authority and will be justifiably cast aside.

> Rise up, O men of God!
> The Church for you doth wait,
> Her strength unequal to her task;
> Rise up, and make her great!
>
> Lift high the cross of Christ!
> Tread where his feet have trod;
> As brothers of the Son of man,
> Rise up, O men of God! [5]

CHAPTER 4

You let fear guide your lives, fear of the unusual, fear of ostracism, fear of punishment, fear of poverty (and riches). . . . You have passed this fear down to your children, but they don't want it! They are learning not to be afraid, of you or anyone. They are learning about what you only talk about: freedom, peace, brotherhood and love.

John Hilgerdt

There is no fear in love; perfect love drives out all fear.

I John 4:18 (TEV)

UPTIGHT OR HANGING LOOSE?

The trustees of a university are meeting. They are looking for a new president. A prominent businessman speaks: "We don't need a policeman; not exactly. But we need someone who can control these kids." Like many of his fellow Americans he is "uptight." He believes Spiro Agnew and Attorney General Mitchell are the finest things President Nixon has given his country. He elects mayors in Los Angeles and Minneapolis. He's grown weary of hippies and pot and Mark Rudd. He reads the *Chicago Tribune,* listens to the morning news, and views his changing world with alarm.

Students no longer sit meekly in their classrooms. Administration buildings are taken over; deans are booted out of their offices; "nonnegotiable" demands are hurled into the teeth of the Establishment; presidents are embattled, faculties are divided, students are marching (or living in "swinging" coed dorms), and older America shakes its head in disbelief.

The black revolution continues to veer toward its separatist goals. Rap Brown's book *Die Nigger Die!* underscores the inevitable hostility of the races. Eldridge Cleaver talks about the black Trojan horse within white America, 23,000,000 strong, just waiting to be unified and organized for the struggle to come. Leroi Jones writes for a black theatre to be performed by black artists for black audiences, and his words are venomous and disruptive. Negroes turn from the churches to the labor unions and expose one more pocket of national hypocrisy. The Kerner Report states the obvious: "Our nation is moving toward two societies, one black, one white." And we grow tense and fearful.

The revolution is not only social, it is moral. Nudity has become the "in" thing on Broadway and in Hollywood. One perceptive young actress says, "I will not undress before a camera. The nude is no longer seen for her beauty, but is exploited for her commercial value." At least hardcore pornography is honest. It doesn't pretend to be anything other than what it is. The undraped body has become the new Statue of Liberty. The four-letter word is the new Declaration of Independence. Hugh Hefner is the Tom Paine of the current American revolution, and the enemy red coat has become the enemy blue nose. The Pill has authored its own emancipation proclamation, and raw sex has emerged as the shared obsession of an age noted primarily for its emptiness, boredom, lack of direction, and loss of faith. Billy Graham declares war on smut, and Bill Coffin confuses the issue by saying, "The church has been concerned about free love—and yet indifferent about free hate." [1] War is a moral question, too.

There has been a loss of faith. Michael Harrington writes, "After God died, Man, who was supposed to replace Him, grew sick of himself. This resulted in a crisis

53

of belief and disbelief, which made the twentieth century spiritually empty." [2] A couple of years ago, in academic circles and in abstract terms, we talked about the "death of God." Today the conversation has shifted to the collapse of the church. If only we could return to the old verities: to the sovereign majesty of God; to the Bible as his inerrant Word; to Jesus Christ, God's only begotten, born of a virgin, crucified for our sins, risen in eternal triumph over sin and death; and to the church as the impregnable fortress against which the gates of hell cannot prevail. But even as we say the words they seem lost in the echo chamber of new images and concepts. How can the rock-ribbed faith of our fathers survive in company with the scientific method, the logical positivism, the relativity and terrifying uncertainty of life in a nuclear age? Contemporary man is uptight. Of course, he is uptight. The German New Testament reads, "In the world you have *angst.*" In such a world, with the tidal wave of radical change surging down upon us all, the believer who stands like some Fearless Fosdick trying to hold back the tide is proving neither his faith nor his courage. He is only revealing his naïveté and inadequate grasp of reality; his impotence in the face of change.

Those of us who seek to be *contemporary* Christians have a choice to make. Will we reflect only the anxieties of the day? Will we be immersed in the angst of the world? Will our stance be rigid, fearful,uptight in the face of what might happen? Or will we possess what the Roman Catholic reformer Hans Küng has called "believing hope." Will we, because of our freedom in Christ, because of the grace given us, be able to hang loose and respond creatively and redemptively to this world in the agony of its present crisis?

While an uptight response to the revolutions around us is understandable, for the Christian it is not justifiable. Students aren't rioting and blacks aren't rebelling *for the fun of it.* Moral values aren't shifting and old beliefs aren't being called into question *by chance.* We live in an age of uncertainty, of unprecedented change, and rigid systems and dogmas will no longer suffice. Back of the forces that threaten and frighten us there are causes that must be dealt with.

In a world that has lived by the sword for thousands of years, and that has known more war casualties in the twentieth century than in all previous centuries combined, war is no longer a permissible luxury; no longer a defensible strategy.

In a world where hunger and starvation are present reality, where two thirds of the earth's people will go to bed hungry tonight, the demand for economic justice will not be silenced.

In a world where colonialism, wearing many disguises, has exploited Asia, Africa, and Latin America, American and European coercive intrusion will no longer be tolerated.

In a world that has bent low under the curse of white racism, the man of color *will* be heard, *will* be freed, *will* determine his own destiny; he *will* overcome.

Yes, and in a world that has heard the church *talk* about love and justice for two thousand years, growing skepticism and indifference demand that we put up or shut up!

Quincy Howe once wrote, "The twentieth century has put the human race on trial for its life." Within this larger courtroom drama the church is on trial for its life—as it should be! The institutions of man are always under the judgments of God and history.

The Pentagon pushes through a multibillion dollar ABM system not to protect our cities, not to protect our people, but to protect our weaponry. We want to maintain a second-strike capacity that can wipe Russia and China off the face of the map. Where is the voice of Christian conscience?

We continue to fight for what we call "freedom" in Vietnam. Freedom? From the first government of Diem in 1954 to the present government of Thieu and Ky, Saigon has been ruled by landowning tax-dodgers who have needed the war to stay in power. Dissent is not tolerated. Buddhists (80 percent of the population) are persecuted. And a nation is being destroyed. Is this what 40,000 American men have died for? Is this what more than a million Vietnamese have died for? Thich Nhat Hanh, the exiled Buddhist monk, referring to the salvation the American military machine has brought to his country, says, "What we Vietnamese need most is to be saved from [your] salvation."

Do you see why students are defying the draft and questioning the war? Why militant blacks are saying that their own freedom, world hunger, and international justice are all bound up together? Why all kinds of people have lost their sense of direction and are seeking escape in cheap pleasure, in sex and drugs and violent retaliation? Do you see *why* the church is on trial? Informed idealism can see right through our double-talk. This is no time for us to self-consciously explain why we are not involved; why the church is not responsive to contemporary need. This is no time for us to be on the defensive; to be uptight. The pressures of history insist that the hour is too late and the needs too desperate for that!

How then can we respond in confidence to crisis? I
know of only one answer. We are called to respond on
the basis of our maturity in Christ; on the basis of Christian love.

You remember Paul's words: "When I was a child, I
spoke like a child, I thought like a child, I reasoned like a
child; when I became a man, I gave up childish ways" (I
Cor. 13:11). Those words are not found in his letter to the
Romans, where the apostle talks about justification by
faith and the spirit-filled life, or in the twelfth chapter of
First Corinthians, where he talks about the church, or in
the fifteenth chapter, where he talks about immortality.
They are at the heart of his incomparable love chapter.
Christian maturity is dependent upon the gift, the sharing,
the practice, and the discipline of love.

In the light of present crisis let me offer a free translation of some familiar words:

"If I speak knowledgeably and with eloquent per-
suasion about world problems, but have not love, I am
bypassing *the* fundamental need. . . .

"If I adopt the stance of the prophet and cry out
against injustice in every form, but have not love, I have
missed the point. . . .

"Or if I embrace the 'theology of hope' and affirm the
sovereignty of God in all of this . . .

"Or if I renounce worldly ambition and materialistic
goals to plunge into ghettoes of poverty and indifference,
if I take pride in my relevant activism, *but have not love, I
am nothing.*"

Agape—God-centered, other-centered, sacrificial
love—is the key to personal wholeness and to the survival
of the race.

The Beatles oversimplified things a bit when they proclaimed in song, "All You Need Is Love." If only it were that easy! But sentiment is not enough. Love must be related to the demands of a very real world. We need to be wise enough to know that there is no deliverance for mankind apart from the complicated structures of his society. Peace is unattainable without the United Nations, World Law, delicate diplomacy, and the radical rearrangement of national priorities. Racial justice requires legislative action, public education, and grassroots participation in the processes of democracy. Where then do Christian love and witness fit into all of this? What is the function of our shared ministry?

Are we not called to be models of the new humanity?

Are we not called to run risks others cannot or will not run? (If not, what is the cross all about?)

Are we not called to use vocation and influence to help direct social change and spiritual renewal?

Are we not called to accept persons, all kinds of persons—the militant and hateful, the old and uncomprehending, the young and arrogant, the "well-fixed" and indifferent—even as our Lord did?

And are we not called to *demonstrate* the love we talk about so easily—to demonstrate it, not simply on the firing line of activism, but with mate and child, with church "boss," with town "bum," and with reactionary antagonist—*for if we have not love, we are nothing!*

Love will turn us away from a rigid and self-righteous perfectionism to a wholesome acceptance of humanity.

It will turn us away from that self-centered individualism that talks about "my" salvation, "my" happiness, and "my" eternal life, that we might respond to the needs of *community* and view ourselves as integral members of a body instead of solo performers.

Love will enable us to see our insecurity for what it really is: uncertainty in the face of the unfamiliar, in the face of personal weakness and pride and sin. Don't you see? To be uptight is to be rigid and self-righteous, a prima donna in a world pleading for true brotherhood; it is to be afraid and uncertain in the face of change. To be uptight is to seek refuge behind the frail walls of an institution when a waiting world is begging for bread and salvation.

But to hang loose is to be free and open, to acknowledge our own humanity and our oneness with the rest of humanity, to take up the towel of the servant and share the burdens of others. To hang loose is to put away childish things and discover the meaning of life in Christ, letting all else fall into place as it will.

"Life in Christ," . . . *in Christ.* There you have it.

Our Lord was the freest of men. His father died when he was but a lad. His mother never fully understood him. He became a popular leader. Predictably the Establishment grew jealous of him, bitterly resented him, and plotted his downfall. Even his friends, faithful and enthusiastic during days of acceptance, fled from his side when storm clouds gathered. People failed him. Religious and political leadership seized him, tried him, and sentenced him to death. His ideals were ridiculed and laughed to scorn. Yet the Nazarene moved from crisis to crisis with magnificent courage and unbelievable calm. How? How can a man be so free, so confident? How can he hang so loose when catastrophe seems imminent? The answer is found in the words of perfect trust spoken from the cross: "Father, into thy hands I commend my spirit." When all else failed, God was there, and hope spoke the final word.

History seems determined to keep the pressure on. Rome, the Sanhedrin, Pilate, Herod, Annas, Caiaphas, Judas, centurions, pieces of silver, and the Place of the Skull are with us yet. They may have new names, but the old forces that corrupt and destroy have not bowed out. "Principalities and powers" would still confine and crucify the realm of the spirit. My word to you is simply this. Don't be intimidated. Hang loose. In the love of Christ and in the freedom of his spirit move into the future unafraid. It belongs to God and you belong to God. "Fear not, for [he] is with you . . . now, and to the end of the age."

CHAPTER 5

[*Black power is*] *the process by which black people and their allies combine their strengths, time and use their strategies to achieve for blacks all the benefits, privileges and options of the society which are open to whites as a matter of course.*

Renewal Magazine

It was for freedom that Christ emancipated us. So stand your ground, and don't let anybody saddle you with the slave system again. Look here, I, Paul himself, am telling you that if you accept segregation, Christ isn't worth a cent to you. . . . Because in Christ Jesus neither segregation nor integration is a determining factor; rather, it is faithfulness activated by love.

Galatians 5:1-4a, 6 (Cotton Patch Version)

CRISIS IN BLACK AND WHITE

In 1964, Charles Silberman wrote a widely read book called *Crisis in Black and White*. Needless to say, it dealt with race relations in America. It talked about identity, power, schools, welfare, and the nature of protest. It was a brilliant study—and that was 1964. Since then fire has raced across the land. Watts, Detroit, Newark, Washington, and Hartford have exploded. Black Panthers have taken to the streets. Cities have become battlegrounds. Malcolm X and Martin Luther King have been shot down. The crisis has become far more crucial.

Most of us are church members. Most of our churches are predominately white. Many of them are saying the "right" things. But where has the church stood in the racial crisis? And where is the Lord of the church? And in the name of that Lord, how are people like us supposed to relate to the most urgent domestic issue of our day?

Leroi Jones, the poet of black protest, speaking to black America, has said, "If we can bring back on ourselves the absolute pain our people must have felt when they came onto this shore we are more ourselves again." Let's go back, in that spirit, to begin at the beginning.

In 1619 the first slave ship came to this shore with its human cargo in chains. In 1715 there were almost 60,000 slaves in the colonies. In 1775 that number had risen to 500,000. By 1830, to more than two million. In 1860, as war threatened to splinter the nation, there were 4,441,000 slaves in the land.

The slave was considered property and treated little better than an animal. He was sold from an auction block. Denied the rights and protections of family life, he was mated as beasts of the field are mated. His worth was based on the strength of his back and the sweat of his brow. He was denied his manhood.

In January of 1863 the Emancipation Proclamation was signed. The black man was "free." There followed no reign of terror; no attempt to avenge 250 years of tragic wrong. But "free"? That's hardly the word.

Reconstruction, with its false hopes and blind inhumanity, brought Jim Crow, the Ku Klux Klan, the lynch law. As recently as 1915 (that is within the life-span of many of us) the state of South Carolina adopted a code for its textile workers that insisted upon absolute apartheid. Black and white workers would use different doorways, different exits, different pay windows, different stairways, different lavatories, different toilets, different drinking buckets and cups and glasses. There would be total separation. Why? Obviously, one race didn't want to be "contaminated" by the other.

During the 1890s, one Negro was lynched every two days in this country. In Waco, Texas, in 1916, a crowd of 10,000 white people stood and cheered as a black mental defective was stabbed, mutilated, and burned to death. Between 1890 and 1950 more than 4,700 lynchings were reported to the federal government. That doesn't take into account Herbert Lee, Louis Allen, three civil rights workers near Philadelphia, Mississippi, Medgar Evers, shot in the back, Jimmy Lee Jackson, four little black girls in a Birmingham church, Martin Luther King—and God only knows how many others. Why the gory details? What right do we have to be spared them? How else can we understand something of the tragedy of the past and the hostility of the present? And it's all based on the accident of color.

Do you know what it is like to be treated solely on the basis of the pigmentation of your skin? Some of you do. Most of us do not.

When you want to buy a house in a "fashionable" neighborhood;
    when you want to apply for a special kind of job;
        when you try to join most private clubs or trade unions;
            when you walk down the center aisle of a proud, lily-white church;
                when you amble down Main Street after dark;
do you know what it's like to be seen first as a black man, and often only as a black man?

Black Like Me is the story of a white man who had his skin chemically treated so he would look black. It worked. He crossed over into the world of hate and fear and hopelessness—the world of the American Negro. He moved from city to city across the southland, accepted as a black man by the blacks; treated as a black man by the

64

whites. He discovered that he was *always* seen in the light of his color. He wrote, "My skin was dark. That was sufficient reason for them to deny me those rights and freedoms without which life loses its significance and becomes little more than animal survival." [1]

Most of us, in our comfortable worlds, don't understand why any white man would want to look or feel like a black man. We live protected lives. Because of this insulation and protection, we have not permitted ourselves to hear the sounds, to see the brokenness, to experience the frustrated anger, the seething passion, the bitter resentment, and the utter defeat of a world not our own.

A Hebrew prophet once said, "I sat where they sat." There is a sense in which this can't be done. There is another sense in which it must be done. Because most of us who are white have not tried to identify with the black man, we have been in no position to relate intelligently or helpfully to the racial crisis. Black anger stands to shout—we turn away. Black anger raises a clenched fist—we tremble and condemn. Black anger lashes out—we judge harshly and strike back. Black anger makes its bold demands—we reject them out of hand. True, responsibility does not condone lawlessness or aimless violence; it does not yield to irrational pressure. But look at the American city, at the American soul, and try to understand! The depraved wrongs of the past have risen up to haunt us. Black anger and separatism are but inevitable responses to white racism. We can elect our law-and-order candidates and praise those who cry "shoot the vandals," but white America is reaping the whirlwind of a blind and brutal past. Five hundred *trillion* dollars would not provide adequate reparation for 350 years of slavery, indignity, and dehumanization.

What then can the church do? It can take its gospel seriously. As Stokely Carmichael once said, "It's time for cats to live what they believe." [2]

The theology of the church is perfectly clear. The church is of God and God is no respecter of persons. He has made of one blood all nations. God is not only color-blind, he is color*less*. He is no more a white God than black, or yellow, or blue, or polka-dot. *God is God!* His love is universal, and is offered to each and all alike. If, as the Bible sometimes hints, God does play favorites, his favoritism is extended to the poor, the blind, the sick, the captive, the outsider. The theology of the church is perfectly clear, but its performance is a different story.

The church, you see, is not a tightly disciplined colony of committed and practicing believers. It is a social institution, reflecting the contradictions and hypocrisy of our culture. It is like Robinson Crusoe's goat pasture. The fences are so distant and the fields so big that the goats inside are as wild as the goats outside.

There is racism in the world? There is racism in the church!

There is segregation in the world? There is segregation in the church!

There has been a betrayal of democratic ideals in our nation? The institution of religion has betrayed its gospel of brotherhood!

But the black-white confrontation, long overdue, may cleanse and purify the church. Albert Vorspan's recent satire "How James Forman Lost His Cool But Saved Religion in 1969" [3] suggests the possibility.

Over the past decade the church has been in agony. Conscious of its past sins and present ambivalence, it is searching its soul. Its voices, though often muffled and lonely, have been heard in Selma and Montgomery and Chicago, on campuses and in halls of state, in community organization and political action, in dreary ghettoes and back-street jungles. Historians will one day look back to the black church as the rallying point for the freedom movement in the South. More and more, the church, (not only the southern black or the inner-city church, but also your church and mine) is getting involved, is committing itself and running risks, is trying to rethink and reenact the place of the cross in the experience of man.

Against this backdrop the church is called to be a classroom, a catalyst, an agent of reconciliation, and an experimental laboratory.

It is called to be a *classroom* where thoughtful people come together to encounter facts, to question civic and church leadership, to discuss issues freely, agreeing and disagreeing in an atmosphere of mutual respect, and to conscientiously relate the gospel of Jesus Christ to social crisis and upheaval.

The church is called to be a *catalyst,* proclaiming and demonstrating the explosive doctrine of love and justice. It is not enough to tolerate change; the church exists to help bring it into being, influence its direction, and bless it in the name of One who promises to make all things new.

It is called to be an *agent of reconciliation,* rejecting racist and Marxist theories of group and class superiority. The church exists to build bridges between pockets of hostility—to break down those walls that too long have separated us.

And the church is called to be an *experimental laboratory.* Our churches are like Macy's display window. The multitudes are passing by and looking in. There is no way to escape their scrutinizing judgment. If the church fails to practice what it preaches, an all-knowing God will condemn it for its cowardly failures, and a cynical world will say, "I told you so. Forget the psalm-singing hypocrites." And history will pass us by.

Today's church is called to be classroom, catalyst, reconciler, innovator; but, above all, it is called to be *the church of Jesus Christ.*

The church belongs to Christ! He is its Lord, and he is the key to the process of change.

Albert Cleage, pastor of the Shrine of the Black Madonna in Detroit, has said, "Black people cannot build dignity on their knees worshiping a white Christ." [4] A thirty-foot mural depicting a black madonna holding a black child stands in the front of his church. Why not? The Oriental painter shows a Holy Mother with slanted eyes and yellow skin. Why not? Churches all over America are cluttered with pictures of a Nordic Christ, a Savior with fair skin, brown hair, blue eyes. Why not? He belongs to all of us in exactly the same way. He is the exclusive property of none of us. "Black theology" is as legitimate as the white theology most of us have taken for granted. When properly formed and understood, it has an essential role to play. It is a theology "whose sole purpose is to apply the freeing power of the gospel to black people under white oppression." [5]

Paul saw Christ as the incomparable unifier of man. One's social status was no longer binding: there was neither slave nor free. One's sex no longer spoke the final word: there was neither male nor female. Racial differences were no longer prisons separating men: there was neither Jew nor Gentile. Why? Because all are *one* in Christ.

The Broadway United Methodist Church of Indianapolis sponsors a club program designed to help elementary school children read, study, work, play, and live together. The clubs meet after school and on Saturday mornings. One afternoon a few years ago, eight little black girls came in and sat down with their group leader. It was spring. It was hot. They were tired of being cooped up in school. They didn't like their teacher, and they talked about her. Finally one of them blurted, "I hate Mrs. So-and-so, she's white!" Then, self-conscious silence. Every little eye turned toward the group leader, who was as white as white could be. There followed a long, long, awkward moment. Finally one of the youngsters said a beautiful thing. Looking straight at her older white friend she said, "Oh, but you're different. You're not white, *you're Christian.*" There you have it! In Christ there is no east or west; no north, no south; no black, no white.

The spirit of the Nazarene is the mortal foe of racism— of any kind. It refuses to be bound by the stupid sins of the past or the cautious compromises of the present. In Christ the least among us—the foulest, the most hypocritical, the most ignorant, the loudest, the smuggest—is seen as a child of God. Christ is our hope, and will be our salvation.

Make no mistake, there is a crisis in black and white. But the church is called upon—and *you* are the church—to *see* the Christ in every man, and to *be* the Christ for every man.

CHAPTER 6

What makes the Christian different from other men?
. . . It is the life described in the beatitudes, the life of
the followers of Jesus, the light which lights the world,
the city set on a hill, the way of self-renunciation, of
utter love, of absolute purity, truthfulness and meek-
ness. It is unreserved love for our enemies, for the
unloving and the unloved, love for our religious, political and personal adversaries. In every case it is the
love which was fulfilled in the cross of Christ.

Dietrich Bonhoeffer

When we allow freedom to ring from every town and
every hamlet, from every state and every city, we will
be able to speed up that day when all of God's children, black men and white men, Jews and Gentiles,
Protestants and Catholics, will be able to join hands
and sing in the words of the old Negro spiritual, "Free
at last! Free at last! Great God A-mighty, we are free
at last!"

Martin Luther King

ACTION AND REACTION

On Sunday, May 4, 1969, James Forman stood inside the chancel at Riverside Church in New York City and read a list of demands. In the name of black America he demanded 60 percent of the church's income from its stocks and real estate. He demanded production control of the church's radio station twelve hours each day. There were other things. Earlier he had asked to speak during the worship service, but his request had been denied. So, at an appointed moment, he and his henchmen stood up and took over. As Forman read his statement, the preacher walked out. So did the choir. So did about two thirds of the congregation. What might have been a history-making conversation between a spokesman for Jesus Christ and a black revolutionary became instead one more tired example of the church's inability to cope with the angry voices and strident demands of the hour.

Much has happened at Riverside since then. There have been congregational meetings and group discussions. Stirring sermons have been preached. (I was there one Sunday when the preacher said that the Black Manifesto might one day hang in an honored place in the church's narthex.) Generous and far-sighted commitments have been made to Harlem and to black America. But so much of it seems to be reaction; self-conscious, over-compensating reaction to charges that were legitimate, to demands that were preposterous, and to an opportunity that went by the board forever.

Has this not been the problem with the Black Manifesto? Because the church has not seized the initiative, has not acted in the name of justice and genuine equality, it is now *re*acting defensively; responding with a strange combination of guilt, anger, embarrassment, and tardy concern.

Bishop Roy Nichols, who is certainly no Uncle Tom, no white man's "patsy," insists that the Black Manifesto called for nothing short of revolution, was Marxist and totalitarian in intent, justified violent intimidation, and was racist through and through, calling for the enthronement of a "black elite." He adds an obvious postscript to his critique. Five hundred million dollars is peanuts; a completely inadequate payoff to the black man when one takes into consideration three-hundred-fifty years of slavery and degradation, and the "unfinished business of black reconstruction left undone after the Civil War." The challenge of reparation and social justice is far too big and costly for the churches of America to handle alone.

But accurate as Bishop Nichol's appraisal may be, history will doubtless take a more kindly view of the Manifesto. Why? Because it reminded the white church of its partnership with those who have enslaved and oppressed, of its apathy in the face of injustice, of its willing participation in a white racist society, and of its selfishness when surrounded by ghettoes of black hunger and black hopelessness. Because the church did not act, it is now being forced to react. This, tragically, is the pattern we seem to live with in the church. We don't change society, we mirror it. We reflect its strengths and its sins; its changing moods and its deep and oft contradictory loyalties.

A critical biographer once wrote that Henry Ward Beecher was "both barometer and record" of his times. "He stood forth a prodigious figure," wrote Paxton Hibben, "not by blazing a path in any wilderness, but by the fact that his inner experience was identical with that of millions of his fellow countrymen." [1] Sinclair Lewis, although he once called Beecher "the archbishop of American liberal Protestantism," argued that he was little more than a real-life version of Elmer Gantry. Lewis said, "[Mr. Beecher] came out for the right side of every question—[but] always a little too late." [2] That's how it's been with people like us and churches like ours. That is why the Black Manifesto is an embarrassment to most of us. It simply reminds us that we weren't there when we should have been, seizing the initiative, blazing the trails, running the risks, acting—not waiting to react, but acting—for the sake of the people and the issues involved.

John Wesley was one of the most influential figures of Western Christianity. Like all great men he has had more than his share of critics. In the 1970s it is relatively easy to draw a caricature of the strange little Oxford don; to talk about his sorry history with women, his theological verbage so unlike our own, his preoccupation with methodology and organization, his weird ideas about witches and the practice of medicine and the eternal whereabouts of dead house pets. But Wesley was a creature of his time as we are creatures of ours. To blame him for living in the eighteenth century is to miss the point entirely.

John Wesley *acted*. He not only reflected his time (as each of us does), he *changed* it. He altered the course of the history of England.

While most of the clergyman of his day were deists—an earlier equivalent of the death-of-God phenomena—Wesley presumed to experience the present, living reality of the divine and to share that reality.

While many of the clergy of his day were wastrels, hunting, drinking and hobnobbing with the landed gentry, Wesley stressed and practiced the disciplines of a personal holiness that seems almost beyond our reach.

While most of the clergy of Wesley's day reflected the snobbish class-consciousness of a well-fixed church, he went to the lowliest of people, brushed the coal dust and the gutter filth aside, and saw the human promise there. He offered a gospel of hope and salvation to anguished souls.

While most of the clergymen of the day gave no thought to prisons and slaves and the travail of a worker's life, the Wesleyan revival gave impetus to prison reform, the abolition of slavery, and the birth and development of the Labor Party in Britain.

John Wesley, unlike Henry Ward Beecher and countless other "popular" preachers, was not content to pamper prevailing moods and sentiments. He defied traditions and challenged bishops; he stirred the conscience and changed the habits of an entire people. He *acted*—in the grace of God and the freedom of His Spirit he *acted*—and a bloodless revolution followed. *One of the reasons the revolutions of the twentieth century seem so chaotic, so random and violent, is because the church has not acted.*

It has belatedly, halfheartedly, resentfully, self-consciously *reacted*. This is what Martin Luther King was talking about, in his letter from the Birmingham jail, when he argued that the church has not been society's headlight, piercing through whatever darkness the future holds. Rather it has been a taillight, rattling along behind, going wherever the momentum of prevailing customs has chosen to take it.

There is a moral freedom, a personal spontaneity in action that reaction denies. Action is human (in the highest sense of the word); reaction is brutish.

Love acts; hostility reacts. Hostility may be a mask worn by fear or insecurity or prejudice. But however rational, however justified the mask appears, the patterns of reaction undermine human values. The patterns are negative and destructive. In foreign affairs, hostility talks about "massive retaliation" (reaction) and "second-strike capacity" (reaction). It tries to isolate "bad" nations and quarantine "bad" ideas by using American tax dollars to build military highways, military arsenals, and military governments in distant places (reaction). At home, hostility sneers and spits, and calls a black man "nigger"; a policeman "pig"; a Mexican "spick"; a white man "honkey" (reaction). It approaches the college campus with mace in hand; the ghetto with gun drawn. It is judgmental and retaliatory. It believes in an eye for an eye and a tooth for a tooth (reaction).

"But I say to you," said our Lord, "it's not enough to react. Love! Function on the basis of love. In the presence of your antagonist have confidence in the power of love. Turn the other cheek. Give him your coat. Walk the second mile. Love even your enemy. Pray for your persecutor. Act like a child of the God who makes the sun

75

rise on the good and the bad alike." Act—don't react—act!

Love acts. Whether it stoops to lift the fallen or reaches out to brush away a tear or enters into dialogue with voices of unreason or gets itself nailed to some cross of infamy, love acts. It is patient and kind; it hopes all things, believes all things, endures all things. It does not fail. Love acts; hostility reacts.

Justice acts; repression reacts. The widely quoted and widely ignored Kerner Report spells out in disturbing detail many of the reasons for racial disorder in America. Among many other factors there have been the repressive tactics of individual policemen and of entire police departments. Police brutality has been a tragic dimension of urban life. Interracial couples are often harassed. Social street gatherings are dispersed. "Aggressive preventive patrols"—roving task forces—move into congested neighborhoods, conducting intensive, often indiscriminate, street stops and searches. And there is the degrading verbal abuse, the spoken word, that can strip a man of his dignity; of his manhood. As the report suggests, this kind of "police misconduct . . . cannot be tolerated." [3] Repression creates civil disorder.

John Rockel is a twenty-six-year-old patrolman in Cincinnati. At one time he was the most hated cop in the black community. He made sixty-five arrests during Cincinnati's June, 1967, riots—twenty of them in one swoop. But that was three years ago. Since then Rockel has studied black history at the University of Cincinnati. He now works in the police community relations division. No longer is he the feared and taunted "pig." Today the city's blacks point to him as the ideal: a cop who really cares.

76

"We have learned by our mistakes," says Patrolman Rockel.[4] Justice is sensitive and enlightened; it acts.

Repression may be a Russian tank rumbling into Prague, or the *Saigon Daily News* being shut down once again; it may be college hotheads shouting down a commencement speaker, or a policeman beating up a reporter in Chicago. However it expresses itself, it undermines community and betrays sacred values.

Too often we have pitted love and justice against each other. We have viewed love as a soft and naïve sentiment; justice as a hard-nosed demand for punishment. Such a division of responsibility betrays the spirit of the New Testament. Jesus was never more just than when he forgave the adulterous woman; never more loving than when he drove the money-changers from the Temple. Love and justice are one. They stand together in defending the weak, challenging the corrupt, forgiving the waylost, and responding with informed compassion to human need. They act in unison.

Faith acts; skepticism reacts. The bishop said, "You preach a horrible doctrine." John Wesley said, "The world is my parish." The one, skeptical of everything the other represented, was reacting. Wesley really didn't care. His faith was responsible for his marching orders and no man's petulant skepticism was going to stand in his way.

Jesus was surrounded by skeptics: a mother, who could not understand; religionists, who resented his unconventional life-style and growing popularity; Judas, who became disenchanted and rebellious; even his closest friends, who denied him because they couldn't be sure of the outcome of his grand defiance and unbelievable self-sacrifice. They sensed his calm, his purpose; but, more important to them, they saw what appeared to be his vulnerability and they reacted. Not Jesus. He acted. On to Jerusalem he went, on before Pilate he went, on to the cross he went—never faltering. The future belonged to God. He belonged to God. The sacrifice was worth making. It was as simple—and as cosmically profound—as that. Faith acts; skepticism reacts.

In these most crucial of times we are called to Christian servanthood. We are surrounded by the forces of reaction. Dare we seize the initiative? *Are we free enough, obedient enough, to act in the name of Christ?*

Some five years ago Louis Lomax, the Negro writer, spoke at the church I then served. Broadway Church was located in the heart of a neighborhood grown black. Lomax talked about the "Protestant ethic" in South Africa and America's Bible Belt. He talked about racism in the churches. Then he turned to me and thanked me for Broadway. With a smile he said, "You folks are leaving churches like this all over the country. You're running away. You're turning them over to us. We're grateful." Later he referred to a conversation he had had with Richard Wright, the novelist, in Paris. Wright, pointing to a cross on a church, had said, "When you see a cross, run. In lands where there are crosses we're called 'nigger.' It's only in lands where there are no crosses that we're called 'brother.' "

When he finished, I responded. Only about 10 percent of us there that afternoon were white. I thanked him for his address (it was penetrating and disturbingly brilliant), saying that people like me needed to hear words like his. But I added two things. First I said, "Forget about taking over this church. We're not about to give it away. It's ours to share. It can be ours together. But no one is giving it to you." Then, pointing to the cross on the altar, I said, "I'm glad you didn't run when you saw that cross. . . . The doors are open here. We're here together. Maybe we're beginning to learn the meaning of the cross."

And maybe we are. Maybe we are. Instead of simply reacting to things that threaten us and defy us, maybe we're learning from Him, who seized the initiative, set his face steadfastly toward Jerusalem, and determined when and where and how he would confront the human crisis. It took a cross. But the choice was his. He acted; that is, God acted through him, as God will act through us—if we are loving, just, and faithful.

CHAPTER 7

I wonder if Jesus knows what's happening on earth these days. Don't bother coming around, Jesus.

Jesus, gold and silver—standing naked in a roomful of modern men. What nerve. Jesus, gold and silver— you have no boots on, and you have no helmet or gun—no briefcase. Powerful Jesus gold and silver with young, thousand-year-old eyes. You look around and you know you must have failed somewhere.

Because here we are, waiting on the eve of destruction with all the odds against any of us living to see the sun rise one day soon.

Joan Baez

Don't let people look down on you because you are young.

I Timothy 4:12 (Phillips)

HALF-PAST THIRTY

John Hilgerdt, a writer for *The East Village Other,* is "most pessimistic about the ability of the Church . . . to bridge the generation gap." In fact, he says, "You *cannot* bridge the gap." That sounds hopeless. Berkeley's FSM cries, "You can't trust anyone over thirty!" and that sounds hopeless too. Especially when you're half-past thirty and want very much to bridge some of the gaps in a segmented society.

Why is it important to build bridges? Maybe Hilgerdt provides part of the answer when he writes, "If [older people] threw their weight with that of their children, they could change the world almost overnight." That fond hope, in itself, ought to justify the effort. But there are more immediate aims. Some of us are parents, public officials, educators, molders of thought, and we *care.*

I am forty-five years of age and the father of five children, plus one—a Turkish "son" who is very much our own. My youngsters are students and married and in the Air Force—and there is a delightful twelve-year-old tagalong. For me to ignore the youth rebellion would be to ignore my own children.

Not only that, but I am the "enemy." What can be more establishmentarian than the bishop of a church? It is assumed that my first loyalties are fiscal and institutional. It is assumed that I am unalterably committed to the status quo. As our friend Hilgerdt writes, "As long as you . . . permit rules and regulations and laws and 'leaders' and standards and codes rather than people to determine our lives you cannot bridge the gap." It is assumed that we are bound by laws, codes, and vested interests.

But I dare not let the young cynic (or the older one for that matter) turn me away. John D. Rockefeller III, writing in the *Saturday Review,* says

There is much to irritate and disturb the older generation. But I submit that we have let ourselves be distracted by the color-ful fringes to the point where we miss the central meaning of today's youthful protest. I am convinced that not only is there tremendous vitality here, but that there is also great potential for good if we can only understand and respond positively.[1]

Milton Mayer confesses, "The young people terrify me." But he adds, "The only hope of the old is the intelligence of the young. Their intelligence may be underdeveloped, but it is not yet corrupted. They are still young."[2]

What is it the young people are trying to say? *They are saying that freedom is as important as their elders pretend it is.* They talk a lot about freedom; about freedom for the black man and the Indian; freedom of choice in Vietnam, freedom from poverty and hunger; academic freedom; about their own personal freedom.

They remind us that this nation was born in a place called Independence Hall and offered "liberty . . . for all." They read in their history books of World War II and

President Roosevelt's four freedoms. They hear a lot of patriotic talk about communist "slavery" and the so-called free world. From childhood on they have heard that freedom is "what it's all about," and they take that concept very seriously. They insist that there is one thing worse than anarchy and that is tyranny.

From time to time this devotion to freedom pits them against authority—parental authority, school authorities, the Pentagon, policemen in Harvard Yard, and the ominous Big Brother who is watching them, whoever he may be.

This really shouldn't surprise me. If memory serves me well I was eleven years old the first time I sneaked out behind the barn to smoke a Marvel cigarette. I was fourteen when I self-consciously slipped into a dingy theatre to watch Hedy Lamarr in *Ecstasy*. I remember the first time I made my mother cry; the first time I dared to argue with my father. I remember the first time I challenged a teacher. I was in the seventh grade. He taught history and it was a presidential election year. Yes, and I remember the first angry letter I wrote a bishop of The Methodist Church. Challenging authority is no new thing.

There is a French parable that tells of a bully and his growing son. The father had intimidated his boy from infancy on. But the boy grew. One day he stood as tall as his father, and, when his father bellowed at him, he struck his father, knocked him down, and dragged him into the vineyard. When they passed the fourth row of grapes, the father cried, "Stop, son, stop! I only dragged *my* father to the third row." This age has no monopoly on rebellion. If you are honest you will confess that in your own individual style you staged your rebellion, you declared your independence and challenged the authority figures in your life. If you did not, you are to be pitied. Rebellion is a natural part of growth.

I wish I could stop there, but *the young are challenging our moral integrity.* Listen to their folk songs and their spokesmen. They accuse us of hypocrisy. Young people argue that while their parents talk about love, integrity, freedom, and fair play, they actually seek material security, comfort, and status. As one old-timer says, "My generation accepted the precepts of its parents. . . . We violated the precepts but we accepted them. The new generation rejects them. . . . We were—and, of course, are—pious frauds. They are impious Abelards." [3] Think of the double standard we impose upon the young.

The young say we praise freedom while berating them for thinking their own thoughts and dreaming their own dreams.

They say we praise democracy while denying them the right to participate in those decisions that will shape their destinies.

They say we speak of love while justifying distant wars and tolerating forms of racism on our own doorstep.

They say we pay lip service to peace while spending seventy billion dollars each year on arms, permitting the Pentagon to influence our national policy to a suicidal extent, and questioning the patriotism or the manhood of those who stand opposed to war.

They say we talk self-righteously about morality while juggling our tax returns, fixing our traffic tickets, cheating on our wives, ignoring the ethical imperatives of poverty, and pretending that mass violence is not violence at all.

They chide us for our alcoholism (it causes 25,000 highway deaths a year), while we outlaw their grass.

Following the sensational coverage of the Woodstock

Rock Festival in the Catskills late last summer a minister-friend wrote Jack Hilgerdt of *The East Village Other* for his comments on the festival, the use of dope, and the generation gap. (As you may have guessed, his reply impressed me.) The *avant garde* journalist was overstating his case a bit when he called Woodstock "the rebirth of mankind," but then he added this sobering word:

Study carefully what Christ had to say and how we live and then tell me who lives closer to the words and habits of Christ. You or us? . . . You really don't think that love and peace and brotherhood and freedom are more than just words. You see these things as "goals" or "possibilities" but never as something available here and now just for the taking.

The judgments of the young may sound harsh and arrogant. Often they are exaggerated. But my generation is vulnerable, and we had better listen, and learn.

The young—and this is the most important thing of all—are seeking meaning in life. *They want to give themselves to worthy causes.* Wasn't it Judge Oliver Wendell Holmes who argued that we either "participate in the passion and the action of our times" or we can be accused of never having lived at all?

Over the past few years I have seen young people on a host of firing lines, participating in the "passion and the action" of their times. During the presidential primaries of 1968 I saw student volunteers working themselves to the point of exhaustion for Bobby Kennedy and Gene McCarthy. Later, I saw young volunteers staffing the offices of the grape pickers' union in Delano, California. I worked alongside college students in urban ghettoes as they tried to teach underprivileged children how to

85

better read and study. I saw the youth participants at the Fourth General Assembly of the World Council of Churches steal the show with their pointed and brilliant contributions. Young people are doing their homework; they are committing themselves; they want to be heard. They see a vision of a better world and are impatient with those of us who shrug and say none is available.

One of the nation's outstanding businessmen, speaking approvingly of the ability and the dedication of the young, recently said, "Many young people are preparing for long-term efforts to change society. For example, the law students of today are concerned less about trusts and estates and corporate law and more about how just the laws are, how poor people and black people can get a better break before the law." [4] I have a young friend who has two graduate degrees. Following the assassination of Martin Luther King, he returned to school, this time to a school of law in Texas, because, he said, recent events had forced him to see the inequities in our system. Too many defenseless people need help for him to remain outside the fray.

This kind of talk may seem strange to some of us, but it indicates responsibilities that are clearly ours. There *is* a generation gap, make no mistake about that. There has always been a conflict between generations. But we can do much to bridge the gap. We can use our age, our experience, our resources, and our influence to help heal a troubled world. We can look upon the dedicated idealism of the young as our natural ally. And (this is the most important thing of all) *we can try to understand.* We can listen. We can be open. We can learn.

On August 8, 1969, Joan Baez sang before 20,000 people in Madison Square Garden. It was a rainy night, but thousands were turned away. At least 85 percent of the audience was under twenty-five. Miss Baez stood barefooted and in a simple dress on a flower-covered circular platform. She said she wanted to turn the huge Garden into a "cozy living room" and she did just that. She talked about her pregnancy (she was expecting a baby in December), about her husband (David is serving a three-year prison term for refusing to comply with the draft), and about an upcoming anti-war demonstration. She allowed time for picture taking and chatted with technicians who were working behind the scenes. And she sang everything from the old IWW song, "Joe Hill," to the Rolling Stones' "As Tears Go By."

The thing that most impressed my wife and me was the religious fervor of the "happening" (and it was that!). These kids may have given up on the church, but they listened in rapt silence as the haunting voice sang, "O happy day! Happy day! When Jesus wash' my sins away." The old gospel song was greeted first with a reverent hush and then with thunderous applause.

The last number of the program—and Miss Baez confessed it was becoming a bit shopworn—was "We Shall Overcome." After listening to several of its many verses we all stood and sang together. Some 15,000 hands went into the air, as fingers formed in the familiar "peace" sign. Emotion took over. It was a camp meeting, an old-time revival, "pentecost with a beat." In that moment the *soul* of young America was bared. It was pleading for human dignity, for justice and peace. It was pleading for, and expressing, love.

In the printed program the dark-haired artist had written:

There is no "Joan Baez, the Folksinger. . . ." [I] sing to you, yes.

To prod you, to remind you, to bring you joy, or sadness, or anger. . . . And I will say . . .

Consider life.

Give life priority over all other things.

Over land.

Over law.

Over profit.

Over promises.

Over all things.

That is the voice of young America. Can we listen? Will we listen? *Dare we listen?*

CHAPTER 8

On a stormy day I walk alone;
My lips murmur your name and the name Vietnam,
And feel close to you in the language of
   our race.
I want to love you;
I want to love Vietnam.
Growing up, my ears are used to the
   sound of gunshots
And explosions of mines.
My hands are without use, as are my lips.
I have all but forgotten the language of
   Man.

Trinh-Cong-Son

This is what the Lord says:
Because of outrage after outrage committed by
   Damascus
I will not relent!
For they have battered Gilead,
They have threshed her with iron-studded sledges. . . .

This is what the Lord says:
Because of outrage after outrage committed by Edom
I will not relent!
For he pursued his brother with a sword in his hand,
He stifled compassion, nursed the anger in his heart,
And cherished his fury.

Amos 1:3, 11 (Phillips)

The jade burned on the mountain retains its natural
   color,
The lotus, blooming in the furnace, does not lose its
   freshness.

Ngo An

LOTUS IN A SEA
OF FIRE

The U.S. Study Team
stayed in the Caravelle Hotel in Saigon. Across the square
was the old Continental. Every night, in the sweltering
heat, hundreds of young Viets rode around the square on
their bicycles and Hondas. Every night the bar girls sat
along Tu Do Street sipping their "Saigon tea." Every night,
off in the distance, one could see and hear the flash and
dull thud of bombs being dropped. This was a nation at
war; long since grown accustomed to war, but at war
nonetheless.

In the suburban slums of Saigon I saw little houses
being built by Vietnamese Christian Services to replace
those demolished by the Tet offensive in 1968. We visited
the An Quong Pagoda. It had been reduced to rubble
during the Tet offensive. One night an enemy rocket

On May 25, 1969, the U.S. Study Team on Religious and Political
Freedom in Vietnam left New York for Paris and Saigon. We returned to the United States on June 9. The team's 36-page report of
findings was entered in the *Congressional Record* of June 17. Members
of the team were: Mrs. John C. Bennett; Allan Brick; Rep. John J.
Conyers, Jr.; Father Robert F. Drinan, S. J.; John de J. Pemberton;
Rabbi Seymour Siegal; Adm. Arnold E. True; and me.

landed east of downtown Saigon, just across the river. That was bringing the war awfully close to a group of relative "outsiders."

Yet nothing—*nothing*—brought it closer than the June 27, 1969, issue of *Life* magazine. It contained the pictures of 242 young American servicemen who had been killed in one week's fighting in South Vietnam. The week was May 28 through June 3, 1969. We were in South Vietnam over that period of time. These young Americans looking out from the pages of a national magazine, some pleasantly, some grimly, had stopped breathing, had stopped *living,* while we went about our appointed task only a short distance away.

As *Life* reminded its readers, it's not enough to know how many died. Who were they? Where did they live? What did they look like? *Why did they die?*

And there is another question; one not often faced by most Americans. What about *the people of Vietnam?* What do they think of this war? What have they been called upon to suffer? How do they regard the carnage?

Their countryside has been laid waste; defoliation and continued fighting have seen to that. Their cities are glutted with millions of nameless refugees. Their family life, the foundation of their society, has been shattered. Last year they suffered more than 200,000 *civilian* casualties. Over a *million* of them have been killed during the past twenty years of unremitting warfare!

Thich Nhat Hanh, fragile-looking little Buddhist monk-poet-scholar, has written a book called, *Lotus in a Sea of Fire.* The "lotus" is Vietnam; the "sea of fire," the war. In it he says the Vietnamese peasants, pathetic bystanders who do not begin to understand the war, are its chief victims. "No one can frighten them with the stories of the evils of communism," he writes. "With their property already destroyed, they do not fear that the communists will take their property. And if one speaks to them of freedom and democracy, they say, 'Of what use is freedom and democracy if one is not alive to enjoy them?' . . . So it is clear that the first problem of the Vietnamese peasant is . . . how to cling to life itself."

I walked through the children's surgical unit of a large Saigon hospital. By my side was a noted physician and former Minister of Education for the Saigon government. He was explaining the things my eyes were seeing. Each year between five and six thousand children are brought into that one unit of the hospital. Of these youngsters 80 percent are war victims. Of the 80 percent, 25 percent suffer from burns. The remainder have been wounded by bomb and shell fragments and other kinds of military hardware. The little amputees were there: a hand gone, an arm gone, no legs. There were little bodies and faces disfigured forever (napalm is an unbelievably vicious weapon). There was the stench of open wounds. These children, none of whom understood communism or capitalism, were the trophies of the kind of war we are fighting.

A group of deputies from the Lower House had a luncheon for us one day. I sat next to a congressman named Duong Minh Kinh. He spoke of the money and firepower being poured into North Vietnam by Russia and China; of the machinery and manpower being poured into South Vietnam by the United States. Then came this poignant word. He said, "We are being made beggars from all of the people of the world in order to destroy ourselves. That is the greatest tragedy of all."

I don't think anyone argues the fact today that the war

has become Americanized. That didn't happen all at once.

In 1950, President Truman threw the full weight of his administration back of the French in the Indo-Chinese war.

In 1954, following Geneva, President Eisenhower supported Ngo Dinh Diem and forsook the guarantees of "free elections,"

In 1961, President Kennedy threw his full support behind a discredited, now-psychotic Diem and increased the number of military "advisors" from 600 to 17,000.

And in 1964 and 1965, all hell broke loose. There was the Bay of Tonkin resolution. We began to bomb the North. The marines landed. Our troop strength was increased from 23,000 to 165,000. No one could question the process of Americanization now as the conflict escalated crazily beyond control.

You know the rest of the story. Today there are more than a half-million American fighting men in Vietnam. We are spending thirty billion dollars a year on the war. We have dropped almost twice the bomb tonnage on Vietnam that *all* the Allies dropped on *all* the enemy during World War II. 40,000 American boys have died. I have already mentioned the Vietnamese casualties.

And *to what end?*

To stop communism, we say. Last year there were far more communists fighting—and with fiercer dedication —in Southeast Asia than there were in 1954. Our escalation was matched each step of the way by counter escalation. Not only that, but our involvement in that war theatre has provided the glue that has held a tottering communist "world empire" together. At the same time, our involvement has sharply divided the so-called free world.

To stop communism—and to defend freedom. Freedom? If the American presence in South Vietnam was securing the happiness and well-being of the people, that would be one thing. If we were honoring the noble traditions of the past and guaranteeing the *freedom* of a people, that would be one thing. But quite the contrary seems true.

Upon our return from Paris and Saigon the study team spent two and a half days on Capitol Hill in Washington. Our first morning there we held a press conference. We offered a summary of our findings: the denial of virtually all procedural protection when persons are arrested; the prevalence of military field courts, extra-constitutional "kangaroo courts" answerable only to President Thieu; and the physical torture of prisoners during periods of arrest and interrogation. Perhaps it was all summed up in one inescapable and conclusive observation: "The Thieu-Ky government relies more upon police state tactics and American support than upon true representation and popular support."

This is nothing new. The Diem government was worse. But the facts make mockery of the freedom we say we represent in Southeast Asia.

For instance, we talked with *political exiles* in France, and there are thousands of noncommunist Vietnamese who are not free to return to their homeland because of their views of the Saigon government or their feelings concerning valid approaches to peace. We talked to Au Truong Thanh, an economist and former Saigon government cabinet member. Alleged to be a "neutralist," he was not permitted to run for the presidency in 1967. We talked to Pham Van Huyen, former Commissioner of Refugees in the Diem government, who was arrested in 1961 and 1963, and then sent into exile. We talked to Thich Nhat Hanh, the Buddist monk, and to many others, exiled because of convictions freely, bravely held. While in South Vietnam we visited the prisons: Con Son Island, Chi Hao, Thu Duc, and National Police Headquarters. We talked to Truong Dinh Dzu, runner-up in the 1967 presidential election. Shortly after the election he was arrested and sentenced to five years in prison. He had advocated negotiations with the NLF. We talked to Thich Thien Minh, second most powerful Buddhist leader south of the 17th parallel. He was arrested on February 23, after criticizing what he called the "corrupt militarism" of the Thieu-Ky government. In the same sermon he scored the "terrorism" of Communism. But that made no difference. He has been held in military custody under tight security since his arrest. He told us, "My only sin is that I believe in peace." We talked with scores of other political prisoners and questioned hundreds of them in groups in the prisons. We were denied access to Nguyen Lau, the owner and publisher of the *Saigon Daily News,* who was being held in the National Police Headquarters when we were there. He has since been sentenced to five years by one of General Thieu's military field courts. We were also denied access to thirteen other prisoners we had asked by name to see.

Although we were told by an official in Washington, before our departure, that we would find no Buddhist monks in the prisons of South Vietnam, we saw 120 of them, in their robes with their shaved heads, in the Chi Hao prison alone. Eighty percent of the people of South Vietnam are Buddhist. Buddhists are, by nature and doctrine nonviolent. The Buddhists, more than others, have suffered the consequences of religious and political oppression.

Censorship was outlawed last year. Since then at least thirty-two newspapers have been closed down by the government.

How can there be freedom; that is, how can there be a truly representative government as long as obvious options are disallowed. When options, in the form of persons, are exiled or imprisoned, there can be no freedom. When options, in the form of ideas, are silenced—newspapers are closed down; student groups outlawed; the expression of critical opinion is not permitted—there can be no freedom. President Thieu stormed into his first press conference following Midway and said speculation concerning a coalition government would not be tolerated by newsmen, by politicians, by anyone. That being the case, what does all this talk about "self-determination" really mean?

Perhaps we are beginning to see light at the other end of the tunnel. Maybe the present administration is daring to run risks and to make decisions its predecessors have not been willing to run and to make. Who really knows?

President Nixon has said his administration is not wedded to the Thieu-Ky government. Time will tell.

He has talked about the imminent withdrawal of 25,000 troops. On January 18, 1969, we had 532,500 men in Vietnam. On August 15, 1969, we had 537,000; an increase of 4,500. Only time will tell.

And if we do withdraw those troops, replacing them with their South Vietnamese counterparts, have we not simply strengthened the bond of tyranny, squeezing the vast majority of Vietnamese nationals into a choking vise between the merciless terrorism of Communism on the one hand and the cynical military corruption of Saigon on the other?

It would appear that we have slowed down our search-and-destroy operations and that Hanoi has cut back its military activities accordingly. Again, only time will tell.

Whatever course we now follow, it should be obvious to the thoughtful, honest mind that there is no simple solution; no easy way out. We can agree with the congressman from Hue who said, "We might all be better off if you'd stayed at home in the first place." We can agree, but the *fact* remains that we are there.

Now the question before the Nixon administration (and each of us) is how to get out with as little hurtful consequence as possible. How can we withdraw while, in the process, attempting to secure the freedom—the true and genuine freedom—of the people involved? How can we help deliver them, not only from Communist aggression, but also from police-state terrorism? How can the stage be set for free elections, so that a viable, *representative* government—not of our choice, but of the choosing of the *majority* of the *Vietnamese* people—will emerge? For in the final analysis Communism will be defeated in Southeast Asia not by bombs or guns or Western diplomacy, but by the *people* of Southeast Asia. They must rally around a cause and leadership of their own and respond to a demonstrably better way!

What can we do? We—sitting here half a world removed from the conflict. There is the stock answer. We can write our congressman; stay in touch with Washington; register our opinions at the ballot box. But there is more. We can support the groups that are constructively involved; the American Friends Service Committee, the Fellowship of Reconciliation, the world peace and social action groups of our denominations. We can try to understand and interpret to others the angry rebellion of youth against the backdrop of the futility of past and present policy. We can share passionate conviction and commitment in our own circles of influence. We can work unashamedly for peace, not for our sakes alone, but for 34 million people 10,000 miles away, who have been torn to shreds by the bestial conflict.

Shortly after returning from Vietnam I spoke about the trip to the Western Pennsylvania Conference of the United Methodist Church. There must have been 1,500 people present. At one point I asked: "Does a sermon like this have any place in an Annual Conference? Is it a sermon at all?" In the back of the auditorium an angry voice cried, "Noooo!" A man was expressing his view. And this was perfectly legitimate. The question had been asked!

But think—

When Amos talked about the "three transgressions and [the] four" of many nations including his own he was cataloging their rapacious conduct in war and their brutalization of persons. Hosea the prophet shook a finger of judgment in the faces of the judges and princes, the insensitive bureaucracy of his land. And, even more important for us, our Lord Christ was called the Prince of Peace. Whether we like it or not, he talked about loving the enemy, feeding the hungry, clothing the naked, visiting the imprisoned; he talked about a cup of cold water, and offered himself for the battered and neglected of his time. He said, "Blessed are the peacemakers, for they shall be called the children of God." Relate those words to present world crisis and to the smoldering wasteland in Southeast Asia.

Our first full day in Saigon was celebrated there, and in many parts of the world, as Gautama Buddha's two thousand, five hundred and thirteenth birthday. We were the special guests of the An Quang Pagoda. As a churchman I was asked to represent our group. At one point in the ceremonies I found myself before an altar, alongside twenty or thirty Buddhist monks, kneeling, shoes off, incense in hand, as Thich Tien Khiet, the old Supreme Patriarch of the United Buddhist Congregation, prayed for his people as "victims of an atrocious war," and prayed for peace. Later I joined the monks in releasing "doves of peace" over the heads of more than 3,000 worshipers. Never have I felt closer to the Lord of life whom I seek to serve; never have I felt more deeply the universal spirit that binds man to brother man and calls us all to forsake the insanity of the past that we might live in unselfish love—as *one*.

CHAPTER 9

Can I, imprisoned, body-bounded, touch
The starry robe of God, and from my soul,
My tiny Part, reach forth to his great Whole,
And spread my Little to the infinite Much,
When Truth forever slips from out my clutch,
And what I take indeed, I do but dole
In cupfuls from a rimless ocean-bowl
That holds a million million million such?
   And yet, some Thing that moves among the stars,
And holds the cosmos in a web of law,
Moves too in me: a hunger, a quick thaw
Of soul that liquefies the ancient bars,
As I, a member of creation, sing
The burning oneness binding everything.

Kenneth Boulding

RACING FOR THE MOON

The moon has always held a strange fascination for man. A clever Associated Press staff writer said it like this:

The moon . . . has been something to change tides by, something to cure warts by, to worship pagan gods by, forecast weather by, dance in the light of by, compose sonatas by, go mad by, make love by, become a vampire by, skinnydip by, make whisky by and wonder how it ever got so high in the sky by. . . . Back before Apollo was a spacecraft, back even before Apollo was a buck-naked lyre-strumming god, man had gazed at the moon and wondered.[1]

He has written songs about it: "Blue Moon," "Moon River," "Moon Glow," "That Ol' Devil Moon." He has waxed poetic. Even Shakespeare, never the simple romantic, warned of its attractive pull: "O swear not by the moon, the inconstant moon, that monthly changes in her circled orb."

Neil Armstrong and Buzz Aldrin landed on the moon on July 20, 1969. Two weeks later, on Sunday, August 3, this sermon was preached in Christ Church (United Methodist), New York City.

101

And yet that inconstant moon, by her very constancy, has been lifted out of the distant skies to become a part of our immediate experience. *Earthlings have landed on the moon, have walked on the moon; in a sense, they have claimed it as their own.*

The conquest of space began long ago in the minds of men like Kepler, Galileo, and Copernicus. Later Jules Verne and H. G. Wells dreamed their dreams. Then came the modern mathematicians: Oberth, Goddard—and the V-2 rocket.

For most of us, however, the space age dawned on one October day in 1957. Oh, we had read our science fiction and followed the adventures of Buck Rogers. We had heard the velvet voice of Vaughn Monroe sing "Racing for the Moon." Now, however, the race was on in earnest. From a site near the Caspian Sea the Russians had launched Sputnik, a 184-pound antenna-rigged sphere, and the chains of earth's gravitational pull had been broken.

The Russians developed a commanding lead in the race for the moon. They put the first artificial satellite in lunar orbit. They were the first to hit the moon with a satellite; the first to photograph its backside. In April of 1961, the Soviet Union sent the first man, Major Yuri Gagarin, into space. And two years later they even sent a woman out. The race was on, but we weren't faring well.

In his acceptance speech following his nomination for the presidency, John F. Kennedy made reference to the "race for mastery of the sky and the rain, the ocean and the tides, the far side of space and the inside of men's minds." And in his state of the union message following his election, Kennedy committed his nation to the goal of "landing a man on the moon and returning him safely to earth" during the 1960s. (Talk about the impossible dream!)

And that is precisely what happened. The Russians got off to a fast start, but slowly we overtook them. Since 1961 there have been thirty-three manned space trips, twenty-one by Americans and twelve by Russians. Then on Sunday, July 20, 1969, we approached the finish line. Two sons of this planet took man's first steps on the lunar surface. We *landed* on the moon, *walked* on the moon, *took pictures* of the moon, *scooped rocks* out of the moon, *planted an American flag* on the moon, and then *returned to earth* safely. The race had been won! (Incidentally, I have never been prouder of my family name than when Neil Armstrong refused to be limited by flag-waving chauvinism and let his first moon-words refer to *mankind's* "giant leap.")

President Nixon, welcoming the astronauts back to earth, called the day of their moon landing the greatest day in history since creation. Maybe in terms of time and space and measurement it was. But beyond quantitative measurements there are qualitative, spiritual realities. On December 25, Christians will remember the birth of their Lord—a rather important day in the history of man. On Easter we will proclaim life's power over death and love's ability to speak the final word. Easter, to the mind of faith, may be the most important day of all. Recently, in Asia, the birthday of Gautama Buddha was celebrated. And there is Bastille Day and Independence Day, and a lot of other days in our common experience that highlight the promise of man's nature and the freedom of his spirit.

Without question man's technological achievements cause him to stand taller today as creative adventurer than he has ever stood before. The fruits of modern science seem more miraculous to laymen like me than ancient stories about the parting of the sea, the stopping of the sun, or the feeding of the multitude. But *in a moment of time drenched with self-congratulations we must beware of the cult of scientism.* Quantitative truth is *not* ultimate, and quantitative achievement leaves much to be desired.

A few years ago I spent several hours with Wernher von Braun at the Space Flight Center in Huntsville, Alabama. We talked about many things: Nazi anti-Semitism and race relations in America; his correspondence with Dr. Albert Schweitzer concerning personal immortality; the most effective ways of combating Communism. Finally, I asked him about the ethical considerations of those who are responsible for the development of modern weaponry. (He, after all, had helped create the V-2 rocket in Hitler's Germany, and has since been America's leading rocket expert.) "How can you sleep nights?" I asked.

"Sometimes it's not easy," he replied. "But you must remember that science only discovers the truth. It is up to others to use it wisely." Technological skills prove nothing save man's remarkable ingenuity. But what he does with those skills will determine the outcome of the human story.

It was in the light of these further considerations that Charles Lindbergh, one of our nation's first space heroes and legends, withdrew from active participation in the ballistic missile program several years ago. In a letter recently published he said:

With Atlases and Titans in position, with Minutemen coming and Polaris submarines under way, I felt that our United States had achieved the indestructible power to destroy any enemy who might attack. But I had become alarmed about the effect our civilization was having on continents and islands, . . . the slashed forests, the eroded mountains, the disappearing wilderness and wildlife. . . . Some of the policies we were following to insure our near-future strength and survival were likely to lead to our distant future weakness and destruction. . . . I wanted to regain contact with the mystery and beauty of nature.[2]

Rodney Johnson, said to be this nation's leading authority on lunar bases, was even more explicit. Warning against the technological pride encouraged by reaching the moon, he argued that such accomplishments must never be permitted to become substitutes for "theological meaning and spiritual expression." [3]

You see, there are abiding values and truths beyond geometric axioms and physical laws. Man's accomplishments, however wondrous, are always under judgment. Not only that; they are always relative and finite.

"In the beginning God. . . ." There is mystery there, the majesty and the mystery of creation.

"And God said, 'Let there be lights in the firmament of the heavens to separate the day from the night. . . . And it was so. And (He) made the two great lights, the greater light to rule the day, and the lesser light to rule the night; he made the stars also.' " (Genesis 1:14-16.) Poetry expresses forms of truth science cannot touch. Don't misunderstand. Science has its essential role to play. But science and technology inevitably move from the known toward the unknown. Again Lindbergh said it:

[Science is] a path leading to and disappearing in mystery. . . . Rather than nullifying religion and proving that "God is dead," science enhances spiritual values by revealing the magnitudes and minitudes—from cosmos to atom—through which man extends and of which he is composed.[4]

Again, the poet has expressed it:

> I have ridden the wind,
> I have ridden the sea,
> I have ridden the moon and the stars.
> I have set my feet in the stirrup seat
> Of a comet coursing Mars.
> And everywhere
> Through the earth and air
> My thought speeds, lightning-shod,
> It comes to a place where, checking pace,
> It cries, "Beyond lies God!"[5]

Of course, there are agonizing problems here. The apostle Paul saw creation pregnant with promise; he saw it "standing on tiptoe" in the presence of its own divine potential. He believed in the ultimacy of God. But he also heard creation's groaning; he saw its pain and its decay. He was a realist, not a romantic; but he was a *Christian* realist. He was convinced of both the misery of man and the grace of God. We are saved by hope, he said, and beyond the travail of the present moment the sons of God will come to know the freedom and the wholeness for which all creation waits.

Now, back to the astronauts. Bill Mauldin may seem a far cry from St. Paul, but there are times when the pen of the political cartoonist becomes almost apostolic. Did you

106

see Mauldin's cartoon in which the astronaut had just returned to earth? He stood by a grease-spattered, patched-together kitchen stove. His exasperated wife, arms waving, shouted, ". . . and I can't get the car fixed, and the dishwasher broke down again, and the TV quit just as you were landing on the moon." That is not the kind of "groaning" the apostle talked about, but it does reflect something of our plight. We can land on the moon, but things here on earth are a mess.

At the very moment Neil Armstrong and Buzz Aldrin were taking their first steps on the moon, I was in a South Dakota church talking about Vietnam. Almost six hundred people were there. We brought a little TV set into the far end of the building, and when something important seemed to be happening we would interrupt the report of tragedy in Southeast Asia with a word of triumph from outer space.

The triumph is real. Caught up in the exhilaration of that triumph both Vice-President Agnew and Wernher von Braun began to talk about landing on Mars. But what about Vietnam and the Middle East, what about the Black Manifesto and exploding campuses, what about crime in the streets, political assassinations and violence as a way of life? While making history on other planets (and spending astronomical sums of taxpayers' money in the process), we may well be losing the battle for a better life here on earth.

We have confused our national priorities. There are fundamental *human* needs that dwarf technological pride and deed. What difference will the conquest of space make if the spirit of man is neglected, if war is permitted to flourish, if poverty and hunger are allowed to continue, if basic rights and freedoms are denied the children of *this* planet? Creation is groaning in agony, and Apollo 11 didn't change that one bit.

I am as proud as any man of the moonshot, but I pray that our national leadership will turn away from its telescopes and scientific timetables long enough to see the human misery on our doorstep.

Richard Feynman, professor of theoretical physics at Caltech, wrote an essay on the relationship of science and religion a few years ago. He called them the "two great heritages" of our civilization. Each is indispensable if man is to continue to grow. Science, with its spirit of adventure into the unknown, has its place. But, wrote Dr. Feynman, so has "the other great heritage . . . Christian ethics—the basis of action on love." [6] Science has spoken, and spoken eloquently, within the past days. Now Christian ethics must reply, gratefully and humbly, but without mincing any words.

Landing hardware on the moon, significant as it is, can never take the place of feeding one hungry child in Biafra, of saving one life in Vietnam, of restoring hope and self-respect to one black or red American, or of bringing a sense of meaning and spiritual fulfillment to one waylost or disenchanted soul.

No one would question the dedicated will, the intellectual and personal discipline, the intensity and enormity of effort required to make possible America's space triumph. The race has been won. But there is more to be said.

Do those of us who name the name of Christ dare stand by in hollow pride and *watch*? This planet groans in agony. But *God is God, and we are his!* As we insist that human beings are more important than mechanical goals, what of *our* dedication, *our* discipline, the intensity and size of *our* effort? We are capable of doing and being so much more than we have done and are. The outcome of our history is involved. Let's get on, then, with the race that is ours, that God's will might be done on earth, even as it has been done in the heavens.

CHAPTER 10

I am told that religion and politics are different spheres of life. But I would say without a moment's hesitation and yet in all modesty that those who claim this do not know what religion is.

Mohandas K. Gandhi

An honorable profession calls forth the chance for responsibility and the opportunity for achievement; against these measures politics is a truly exciting adventure.

Robert F. Kennedy

THE CHRISTIAN
AS POLITICIAN

The last three weeks before the election in 1968 promised to be among the most intense and frightening in America's political history. In such a heated moment perhaps the safest name that could be called to mind would be that of Calvin Coolidge. President Coolidge once said, "America was born in a revival of religion. Back of this revival were John Wesley, George Whitefield, and Francis Asbury." "America was born in a revival." I am certain most scholars would take issue with that relatively simple explanation of our national beginnings. Even so, there is no question but that Puritans and Separatists in New England, Catholics in Maryland, and Quakers in Pennsylvania, Roger Williams, Ann Hutchinson, George White-

This address was delivered on October 15, 1968, to a group of United Methodist ministers at the Kansas Pastors' School. The personal testimony appearing on pages 116-19 would not be a part of a sermon shared with a typical congregation. I agree with those who insist that partisan politics seldom if ever belong in the pulpit. These words were spoken to colleagues and were intended to illustrate a style of valid contemporary ministry.

field, Francis Asbury, and other deeply religious people who were seeking a greater degree of personal and group freedom helped give shape and character to these United States. To divorce the political realities of this land from their religious foundations is like trying to rip a tree from its roots. There is a sense in which Coolidge was right. The Wesleyan revival was something of a midwife in helping bring this nation to birth.

But John Wesley once said, "We have nothing to do but save souls." What do you make of a statement like that? Doesn't that, in effect, tell us that Christians should stay away from public controversy and political judgment? We have nothing to do but save souls, he said. Don't lightly dismiss the comment! *With politicians manipulating us, headlines screaming at us, and current events obscuring our vision of things abiding and eternal we can, too easily, lose sight of the primacy of the person.*

In the spring of 1968 I attended the Uniting Conference of my denomination in Dallas. I went with misgivings. I assumed that we would be asked to squirt a bit of lubricant on the ecclesiastical machinery of the EUB and Methodist denominations as they came together. I was wrong. Dallas was exciting; it proved to be far more than the structural merger of two churches. There was a new mood abroad. There was impatience with outmoded forms and irrelevant answers. There was a determination to be the church; not a cozy nineteenth-century institution, but a New Testament church preparing for witness and mission in the twenty-first century. Yet everything seemed to be done under a shotgun of current events. We debated Vietnam, civil disobedience, selective conscientious objection, the urban crisis, poverty, black power, and white racism; we talked about the posture of the church in the presence of the here and now.

On the way from the auditorium to the hotel one night I fell into step with a fine young physician from Minnesota. He was disturbed. He was a devout conservative, who longed to hear some word of personal assurance. He said, "I need to hear someone say that Christ died for me, to save me from my sins." And he was right! In such a moment of time we must blend the personal resources and social implications of the faith. We might not say it like the young doctor. But we need to know that God cares about us; that the Infinite Beyond is, in some mysterious way, related to, and a part of, our most personal worlds.

There is nothing to be gained by returning to the tired controversies of the past, to the fight (and there is no other word for it) that raged between a rock-ribbed fundamentalism and a much too shallow modernism, between an overly optimistic social gospel and an utterly self-centered personal gospel. The hour is too late and the needs too sobering for that!

The most impatient among us must acknowledge that the gospel of Jesus Christ offers strength to the broken, forgiveness to the wayward, hope to the distraught and the cynical, new life to the empty and the lost. The gospel is a *personal* gospel, make no mistake of it.

But we are here to talk about the Christian as politician. The same Wesley who said "We have nothing to do but save souls" said, "I have no religion but a social religion; I know no holiness but social holiness." The Wesley who said "I am a man of one book" (the Bible, of course) also edited several volumes of English history, wrote on medical practices, and was well acquainted with the broad sweep of England's culture in his day. And the Wesleyan revival made a unique contribution, in England, to the abolition of the slave trade, prison reform, and the birth and development of the Labor Party. David Lloyd George once said, "Methodism . . . has given a different outlook to the British and American. . . . John Wesley inaugurated a movement that gripped the soul of England."

You see, there is no way to divorce faith from life; the gospel from the world; the church from politics. At least there is no legitimate way. *Politics is an essential province of Christian concern.*

Politics—what is it? The dictionary says it is the "science and art of government." And what is government? It is the exercise of administrative power over people. Politics, then, is the science of administering the public affairs of people. Or, as the Greeks defined it, it is "the art of making and keeping people truly human." What could be more closely related to the practice of the faith?

The Bible does not deny the centrality of such matters. It is cluttered with political images and symbols: covenants, kingdoms, laws, rulers, judges. Joseph served as the "prime minister" of Egypt. Moses challenged his government and led a slave revolt. Saul, David, and Solomon were kings. Micah cried out against the corruption of princes and their policies. Isaiah, the most political of the lot, moved in and out of affairs of state influencing the reign of King Hezekiah as no other man. And don't lose sight of Jesus and the beautiful balance he maintained between the sacred and profane; between the religious and the worldly. Jesus was no ordinary rabbi. He was the unexpected presence in the marketplace. In his first public statement his words embraced the poor and the captive. In one of his last utterances he judged those nations—political units—that were blind to the needs of the hungry, the thirsty, the naked, the sick, and the imprisoned; the outsider. Jesus was put to death, not because he was a wonder-worker healing the sick, but because he was a prophet disturbing the status quo, refusing to bend his knee to a Pilate and a Herod. The chain of events leading to the crucifixion was far more political than religious.

We have all heard the words "You fellows ought to stop meddling in politics and stick to preaching." How different our world would be had Moses, Amos, Isaiah, Jesus, Paul, John Calvin, John Wesley, Martin Niemöller, Dietrich Bonhoeffer, Mohandas Gandhi, and Martin Luther King heeded those words. If we are committed to the welfare of people, and seek to be faithful to Christ in *all* things, there is no way we can withdraw from the stress and storm of a very real world. If politics is the art of making and keeping persons truly human, then *the Christian has undeniable rights and responsibilities in public affairs.*

To argue that the Christian is, by nature, a politician does *not* mean that the church should be turned into a political animal; turned into a pawn on some Machiavelli's chessboard. It is not the function of the church to speak ex-cathedra on every controversial issue that comes down the pike, to endorse candidates and promote partisan platforms. The church is not here to respond to candidates on the basis of partisanship in the name of expediency. It is here to respond to issues on the basis of principles in the name and spirit of Christ.

There are certain all-important, fundamental issues

confronting the human family today. There are the issues of international anarchy, national arrogance, nuclear weaponry, and world peace. There is the technological revolution: cybernetics, automation, the use of leisure time, and the training (perhaps the saving) of the unskilled worker. There is the urban revolution with its ghetto slums, its pockets of poverty, its racial explosiveness and human hopelessness. There is national morality: the preservation of the family, law and order, ethics in government, and personal discipline. You can draw up your own list: fair employment practices, open housing, taxation, space exploration, freedom—human freedom.

One of the responsibilities of the church is to help both congregation and community explore such issues in the light of Christian values. *The Christian will study the issues* and make his political judgments on the basis of New Testament insight and devotion.

He will vote (that goes without saying). He will take ward and precinct politics, local contests and primary elections as seriously as he takes the national quadrennial melodrama. Far more than most of us realize, freedom is secured or lost, justice is enhanced or betrayed, and national directions are determined at the grass roots.

But it is not enough to simply study, think, and vote. If democracy is to be strengthened *there must be personal involvement.* And involvement brings with it inevitable frustration. Let me give my "personal testimony."

I am one of those who is unalterably opposed to our nation's military presence in Vietnam. Our policies there have not only backfired; they have denied our best traditions, betrayed our national idealism, and have sought to impose our political notions and way of life on a distant people. More than one million Vietnamese lives have been lost over the past twenty years as Frenchmen and now Americans have unilaterally without international approval waded into the jungles of a faraway land. Forty thousand American servicemen have been slain in a war that is probably none of their business.

I am one of those who believe that the political institutions of this republic need to be cleansed; that the prevailing "establishments" of the country need to be redirected by a new kind of politics.

So when Al Lowenstein flew into Indianapolis one freezing December night I was one of a handful of men who met him in a bank basement to found "Hoosiers for a Democratic Alternative." I became vice-president of the statewide organization. Later, when Senator McCarthy announced for the presidency, we threw our full support to him. I became a state coordinator for the Minnesota senator, introduced him at Hoosier rallies, and was with him in his hotel suite as the Primary returns rolled in in May.

I was one of the few in his camp who rejoiced when Senator Kennedy announced, for I frankly doubted Senator McCarthy's ability to pull things together in Chicago. We needed the political muscle of the Kennedys; their know-how and their incomparable brain-trust. My wife became a block captain for RFK. When he was slain our eleven-year daughter removed the "Snoopy for President" banner from her bedroom wall and replaced it with a portrait of Robert Kennedy. As a family we were involved.

Do I need to tell you of the frustrations?

There was Chicago. Forget the hippies, the yippies, the police, and national guardsmen. Without question there

117

was a vast and articulate mood of dissent in Chicago. It was silenced as an omnipresent "machine" prevailed. Mayor Daley nodded and microphones went dead; Mayor Daley nodded and meetings were adjourned; Mayor Daley nodded and his "hired hands" in the balconies whooped and hollered; Mayor Daley nodded and a presidential candidate was selected. This was not democracy; it was the naked power of bossism.

Miami Beach was not much better, it was just a lot nicer. If Chicago had its Richard Daley and John Connally, Miami Beach had its Strom Thurmond. The Republicans had a smooth operation, bloodless and utterly innocuous, a PR man's dream. No stands were taken. No debates were encouraged. We only heard the reassuring tones of a "manufactured" candidate comfort us by saying, "Elect me first, and *then* I'll tell you what I'm going to do."

Then came the ultimate absurdity—George Wallace. George Wallace, we were told, would draw nearly 20 percent of the votes cast. I have seen the state flag of Alabama fly over my nation's flag on the capitol building in Wallace's Montgomery. I have seen newsreels showing this champion of law and order defying federal marshalls on the campus of the University of Alabama. Education is an absolute "must" in today's world, and Alabama's per capita investment in public education is the lowest in the nation, with one or two possible exceptions. Our nation is dangerously split, and Mr. Wallace said that he would drive his car over the form of a protesting student. He once said he would never be "outniggered" again. George Wallace selected as his running mate a retired general who said there is no difference between nuclear and conventional weaponry, and who once argued that Vietnam ought to be bombed "back into the Stone Age."

George Wallace, the man who one out of six Americans would see in the White House as the most powerful man in the world. My God! Do you know the most frightening aspect of it all? Wallace's major strength was drawn from across the so-called Bible Belt. Those who voted for him wore more Sunday school pins, quoted more Bible verses, sang more gospel songs, and prayed more pious prayers than those who supported the "regular" candidates. Don't blame George for that. But what a commentary on the kinds of evangelism and churchmanship that refuse to become involved in political process and decision.

Involvement brings with it frustration. But I have no right to ask others to accept civic responsibilities I am not willing to assume. I have no right to ask others to run risks I am not willing to run. I have no right to tell others to become involved if I protect myself by trying to remain detached and aloof. I do not suggest that you do as I have done. Each of us must work out his own patterns of obedience. I do insist, however, that the Christian (and this includes the clergyman) has an obligation to relate himself to those areas of decision-making where community policy and life are formed.

We will not always agree on issues and candidates, but as individual Christians—*not as a church, but as individual Christians*—we are challenged to enter the rough-and-tumble arena of human activity where the earthbound destiny of a people is determined. Politics is dirty only if people like us let it become dirty. It is up to us to clean it up that it might attract the brightest and most idealistic of our young.

Beyond encouraging personal involvement what can

119

the church do? *The church can enter into mission on the basis of human need.* The day of pious resolution and homiletical pronouncement has long since passed. The church exists to *live* the Word; to *do* the truth. The World Council of Churches has said, "Everything the Church *does* is of evangelizing significance. Through all of the aspects of its life the Church participates in Christ's mission to the world." Not those who say "Lord, Lord"—those who say and sing and preach the right words—but those who *do* the will of God belong to his kingdom. The church, as it moves beyond its walls to respond to the cry of humanity, is doing what Jesus did in the marketplace.

When the church opens its doors to Head Start classes and to Scout troops, it is helping prepare young people for a more creative and secure future. When the country church interprets the nature of change to its people, and when it opens its doors to Future Farmers and home demonstration agents and agricultural experimentation projects, it is helping to redeem its surroundings. When the city church rolls up its sleeves and attempts to do something about rat-infested slums, open housing, police brutality, crime in the streets, equal employment opportunity, and racial discrimination, it is functioning as the servant church. The church always has political significance. When it hides behind its doors, it is significant for what it fails to be and do. But when it goes out into the world, with towel in hand, to serve, it is being faithful to the One who gave himself for the least among us. That is significant, too.

Aristotle said, "Politics is the art of making and keeping people human." Church fathers said it is the "function of the gospel to help persons become truly human." When

120

they are true to their highest insights, politics and religion are one in seeking to build a "new humanity." Let the Christian then be a politician in the best sense of the word. Let him be faithful to the Christ, who was willing to die that man might be free and that this earth might be a fairer place on which to live.

CHAPTER 11

"But the tree's been cut down," gently Bruce told his father.

"I know it is down. But the stump is there. The stump will put out new shoots and the Tree will come back. Ay, son, it has a deep tap root. It goes down into the land. Deep down. The tap root has not been killed, and until the tap root dies, a tree is never dead."

James Street

rad'-i-cal 1. Of, pertaining to, or preceeding from the root. 2. Original, fundamental; reaching to the center of ultimate source.

Webster's New Collegiate Dictionary

Look to the rock from which you were
   hewn,
And the quarry from which you were
   dug.

Isaiah 51:1 (Goodspeed)

RADICALISM
RECONSIDERED

I am a radical; at least I try to be. To begin like that requires an explanation. When I mention radicalism, there are certain things I am *not* talking about.

I am not talking about the radicalism of black revolution, though I wish its unthinking critics would take the time to read, with open mind, Stokely Carmichael's *Black Power,* Cleaver's *Soul on Ice* and the *Autobiography of Malcolm X.*

I am not talking about the radical right, though I devour each issue of the *National Review* and find William Buckley stimulating and provocative.

I'm not talking about the radicalism of the New Left, though its elder statesmen, Michael Harrington and Jack Newfield, have much to say to us about the crises of our time.

I'm not even talking about theological radicalism. I

This sermon was delivered to a group of clergymen at the Texas Pastors' School on July 9, 1969. This accounts for its references to ministers and their particular problems.

have read Gabriel Vahanian and Bill Hamilton with personal profit—but, to each his own.

I am not talking about doctrinaire radicalism, about the radicalism of manifesto and scholarly treatise. I am talking about a personal, existential radicalism that relates the *me* of a given moment to the *this* or *thou* of that given moment.

The word "radical" frightens people. Yet it means "fundamental" (a shocking thought to some of my Fundamentalist friends). It refers to bedrock basics. *Radicalism needs to be reconsidered, for it calls us—by definition—to the roots of our faith.*

As a United Methodist I am in the tradition of John Wesley. I am convinced that most of us have overlooked the essential genius of the man. We have been so impressed by his warm heart and his talent for organization that we have lost sight of his relevance for the contemporary church.

To take seriously his *reliance upon the Word of God;* to take seriously his *experimental theology* that both justified by faith and perfected in love; to take seriously the *breadth of his scholarship* and his insistence upon regulated study; to take seriously the *disciplines of his personal life* that enabled him, as much as any figure of the eighteenth century, to gain maximal results from the raw materials of his being; to take seriously the *simplicity and frugality of his life-style,* his utter selflessness; and, to take seriously his *ardent desire to reach and reclaim* the coal miner and the field hand, the least among men—is to return to the virgin soil of Methodism's birth and to a repository of neglected ecumenical insight.

Yet John Wesley would be the first to say, "Don't stop

here. The roots go deeper than this." I studied with Carl Rogers when he was still at the University of Chicago. It was at a time when his client-centered therapy was riding the crest of a wave and you were either "Rogerian" or "anti-Rogerian." Rogers was fond of puzzling his students by saying, "I am not Rogerian." In that same sense, Wesley was not "Wesleyan"; he was Christian.

Wesley would insist that the Christian radical needs to trace his roots back, back, back, through Luther and Calvin, Aquinas and Augustine, the church fathers, back over the terrain of the New Testament into the presence of the Savior of men and the Lord of history. *Christ represents the taproot, the true radicalism, of the faith.*

If the church is to be reshaped or reborn or renewed (call it whatever you will), if it is going to be—*in fact*—the church of Jesus Christ, then it must return to its Galilean roots to draw strength and grace from the source of its being. It was T. R. Glover, the church historian, who said flatly and simply: "We are not making enough of Jesus Christ." [1]

Christian radicalism involves *radical surrender.* Albert Outler reminds us that "faith is either in dead earnest or just dead." [2]

Do you remember the old invitation song:

> I surrender all,
> I surrender all.
> All to thee, my blessed Savior,
> I surrender all.

How many times as a new Christian and young preacher I sang those words! And they convey the exact meaning of what I am talking about. Leave the noise and the sweat of the country revival and that total surrender is Kierkegaard's "leap of faith"; it is Tillich's "ultimate concern."

Fifty years ago a young American Communist, forsaking the relative comfort of his former way of life, cried, "I must fling myself into the cauldron of world revolution." That is the abandoned commitment that has made Che Guevera the martyr-hero of the young. By training he was a physician; by profession, a revolutionary. When the fighting died down in Cuba and Castro seemed secure, Guevera moved on into the mountainous jungles of Bolivia, to be sought out and shot down as he tried to extend the boundaries of the revolution. The twentieth-century revolutionary, whether his name is Lenin or Trotsky, Stalin or Tito, Mussolini or Hitler, Castro, Che, Mao, Ho, or Huey Newton, *expects* to be hunted down, *expects* to be imprisoned, to be martyred, even as he flings himself into his cause and gambles on the outcome of his sacrifice.

And we are told morale is low in the ministry. Why?

Well, you know how appointments were made at Annual Conference and who got what. You know what the pension plan is. You know how slow and crippling advancements are and how our talents go unrecognized. The last time Smith moved, his wife had to give up her job and they had to buy furniture for the parsonage, yet payments on the two cars went right on. (*Really.*) I have no right to say a word! As a bishop of the church—and as a "successful" pastor before that—I haven't been forced to make a *New Testament* sacrifice, for a long, long time.

The Paul who was sent to prison for Christ's sake, who was stoned, beaten, misunderstood, driven from town to town, and finally martyred for Christ's sake, did not resent the hardship; rather he counted it a privilege. "For me to

126

live is Christ," he said; "to die is gain." That is the radicalism of surrender.

Jesus approached those rugged fisherman long ago and cried, "Follow me." And "fools" that they were, they left their nets and followed. *They left their nets*—that's what it took.

I don't know what your nets are—

ego needs that won't quit;
cruel neglect of wife and children;
laziness that limits your potential;
a sycophant's security in a well-fixed church;
preoccupation with "success" that loses sight
of people and of mission;
relationships and habits that can't be aired
to public view, but need to be confessed
and forgiven—

I don't know what your nets are, but when our Lord says "leave your nets and follow," he is saying "get rid of that excess baggage; cut off those attitudes, relationships, and motives that will betray you; get off that hub of self-centeredness about which your interests and loyalties have revolved, and follow me."

We can cling to our nets and forfeit our true humanity (our salvation, if you please). Or we can leave them behind, as did the disciples of old, and find new life and purpose in surrender to the historic fact and living experience of Jesus Christ.

But the radicalism of surrender, the radicalism of a Galilean lakeside, a Damascus Road, an Aldersgate prayer meeting, is not enough. The disciples left their fishing boats and walked by their Lord's side, however hesitantly and falteringly, to the place of the cross. Paul fought his good fight, kept his faith, and finished his arduous course. And Wesley left Aldersgate for the mine shaft and the open field. Beyond the radicalism of surrender is *the radicalism of concerned response.*

A part of the youth revolt is a rejection of those persons and institutions that give lip service to lofty ideals and noble causes, but that stop short of putting life on the line for the things they talk about. Within the framework of their biases and limitations these youngsters have done their homework. They know a good deal more about Vietnam, draft laws, black self-consciousness, the Pentagon, and the distribution of wealth and power than most of us. And they are impatient with people who talk grandly about brotherhood and peace, but who haven't bothered to learn the rules of the game and the names of the players; who have made little effort to leave the security of the grandstand and get down on the playing field where the future of mankind is being ground out.

I would not romanticize this thing of involvement. It is a "mixed bag." After returning from Vietnam, I spent some time in Washington. Every Wednesday, Quakers were gathering on the Capitol steps to read the names of the war dead and be arrested. I had heard about their sober exercise and, in spite of Speaker McCormick's aversion to it, I thought I saw its purpose and legitimacy. I had been a member of an American team studying religious and political repression in Saigon; and silencing the Quakers was repression here at home. Walking in front of the Capitol one particular Wednesday noon, I saw the small band of Quakers reading the names. Curious, I mounted the steps to listen and to watch. A congressman friend from Indiana joined me. Soon two more congressmen were there. Then a police captain appeared out of nowhere, bullhorn in hand, and told us to be gone within five minutes or to face arrest. That which began as an expression of curiosity suddenly became a cause. This was *my* Capitol. These Quakers were exercising their constitutional rights calmly and with dignity. (In Indiana, newspapers had commended the John Birch Society for doing exactly the same thing, and two weeks later *Life* would do it with pictures and receive an unprecedented mail response.) I stayed.

Well, to make a long story short, the Quakers were arrested. The congressmen, immune to arrest on the Capitol steps, continued to read the names. Though I got as far as the paddy wagon, I was spared. It seems that Quakers were in season, but the authorities didn't want a United Methodist bishop on their hands.

My feelings were mixed. On the one hand, I've never been in jail. I didn't go to Selma; I wasn't in Mississippi for "freedom rides"; I haven't encouraged the burning of draft cards. I wondered—what will my grandchildren think of a grandfather who lived in this country in the 50s and 60s and was never put in jail, not even once, for race or peace?

But, on the other hand, I could see good, devoted hardworking laymen in North and South Dakota, unable to understand or accept my action. Some of them would be deeply offended, and it would affect their attitudes toward the church. True, Jeremiah, Socrates, and St. Paul were jailed—but that was long ago, and they didn't wear sideburns (they wore whiskers instead).

I confess (and it *is* a confession) I was relieved. I had been true to my ideals without being carted off to prison. Anyway, the Quakers were getting along very well without me, thank you.

The incident, however, helps bring into focus certain implications of concerned response; of radical (remember the dictionary definition) involvement. Before romping onto one of several available and obvious battlefields, the Christian who wants to be obedient and faithful should ask some searching questions.

Is sound judgment a part of my response? What is the role of the radical Christian in this situation? Is this where I ought to make my witness, or are others more qualified and better able to serve here? What are the issues at stake? Am I being impetuous and immature in my responses, or am I reflecting sound reasoning as well as commitment? Do I understand the probable consequences of my actions and am I willing to accept them?

Are my motives "Christian"? In the fall of 1969, in Minneapolis, Billy Graham held a press conference. He told newsmen that there are many people "who want to be involved in social action today not because they're concerned with their fellowman, but because they want to be where the action is . . . and where the cameras are." [3] (Strange comment coming from the most widely publicized and oft photographed religious leader of the century.) I have no right to question the motives of my fellows. I have a sacred obligation to be honest with myself. Am I genuinely concerned about my fellowman, or am I—for whatever neurotic reasons—determined to "do my own thing"? Am I seeking the spotlight and personal honor, or am I offering myself, however inadequately, to meet desperate human need?

Am I willing to go wherever I feel led? We have mentioned the disciples, who left their nets; Paul, who endured to the end; and Wesley, who left the warm assurance of Aldersgate to face personal abuse and public scorn across his homeland. The radical Christian is often called upon to pay dearly for his faithfulness. Today Broadway Tabernacle in New York City looks run-down and neglected. Long years ago, Joseph P. Thompson brought unusual distinction to its pulpit as he spoke to the urgent issues of his day. On one occasion an enraged listener shot at him from the balcony. Thompson didn't even duck. He simply said, "The man who stands in this pulpit must be the first to see, the first to feel, the first to move against all forms of moral evil in the world." [4] That is the radicalism of Christian servanthood.

As for the institutional church, all of it can go if none of it serves today's needs. The only things that need to be conserved are the things that can be used. . . . Today, any lucid person in Jesus Christ understands that there are two alternatives relative to renewal of the Church. One is that the Church has been said "No" to by God. . . . The other is to believe that the Church is renewable from within.

Joseph Mathews

Hezekiah . . . did that which was right in the sight of the Lord. . . . He opened the doors of the house of the Lord and repaired them. He also brought in the priests and the Levites, and assembled them in the open square on the east. Then he said to them, "Listen to me, O Levites; sanctify yourselves and reconsecrate the house of the Lord . . . and carry out the filth from the holy place."

II Chronicles 29:1-6 (Goodspeed)

God is working his reconciliation in the world. It is the world's renewal in which the church is privileged to participate.

Harvey Cox

RENEWAL:
IMPERTINENCE OR
IMPERATIVE?

In the popular mind "evangelism" and "revivalism" are one, and revivalism recalls images of brush-arbor camp meetings and Billy Sunday antics. It brings to mind invitation hymns, sawdust trails, cottage prayer meetings, and preachers with loud sandpaper voices and prominent jugular veins. It is a relic of the past. "Renewal" is the word in current vogue. Yet today's renewalist has much the same zeal and single-minded dedication that the old-timer had, who sang "Revive Us Again" and prayed through half the night.

Renewal is suspect in some circles simply because, like every movement, it has its bizarre fringes and phony harbingers. Renewal means different things to different people.

To some it is Vatican II, the ecumenical movement, and biblical theology.

To others it is Father Groppi leading his marchers in Milwaukee and black preachers kneeling on courthouse steps in Mississippi.

It is liturgical. Canon Southcott says, "Renewal means

the rediscovery of the meaning of worship . . . the rediscovery of the meaning of the Eucharist." [1]

Renewal is community organization. It is the irreverent relevance of the Ecumenical Institute, and Saul Alinsky organizing somebody's hostilities in somebody's neighborhood someplace.

It is Keith Miller's *Taste of New Wine* and Billy Graham preaching to a stadium full of people or praying in President Nixon's White House.

It is Malcolm Boyd's "underground church." It is Dietrich Bonhoeffer, Abbe Michonneau, Stephen Rose, and Hugh Hefner; the "new theology" and the "new morality," with guitars strumming all over the place. It is Joan Baez sending her husband off to jail for resisting the draft.

Renewal means prayer and Bible study groups, lay witness missions and sensitivity training.

Or is it nude dancers cavorting before a strange assortment of worshipers in Greenwich Village?

Again, renewal means different things to different people. Yet the many facets of the movement appear to have certain characteristics and impatient concerns in common. *There is a boldness about the movement; a boldness bordering on arrogance, bordering on impertinence* Renewalists accuse the church of entertaining a random variety of heresies and sins.

They charge that the church, as most of us have known the church, is not a divine creation; it is a middle-class institution defending a WASP value system that stubbornly opposes every form of change.

They charge that the church, as most of us have known the church, has become a defender of the American way of life, more concerned about free enterprise, stopping communism, and supporting the local police than with a demanding gospel of love and justice, and a cross-centered approach to involvement in human affairs.

They charge that the church, as most of us have known the church, is hung up on statistics. How big is your church? Do you have a new and comfortable building? What is your budget? How many new members did you "take in" last year? Can they pay their own way? Are they "quality" folk?

It is at the point of church membership that the renewalists grow most indignant. They charge that joining the church is like joining the garden or civic club of your choice. Believe what you choose, live as you choose, think and do what you will, but attend as you can and help pay for the air-conditioning. ("Worship in air-conditioned comfort" seems to have supplanted "Come to Jesus" as the most persuasive invitation of the day.)

What are the charges again? The church is a middle-class institution; it is more concerned about the American way of life than the gospel of Jesus Christ; it is preoccupied with its institutional strength and survival; and (as if we needed more) church members are an uncommitted and undisciplined lot; a congenial band of flabby pretenders. *Talk about impertinence!*

And yet, let's face it, there is disturbing truth in all of this. Is the church as you know it a reflection of the will, the spirit, and the sacrifice of Christ? Men like Harvey Cox argue that traditional religion has collapsed and preaching is an irrelevant art; we should turn away from church-centered worship, they say, and follow our Lord into social service and political action. And these men are so glib and dogmatic. Their voices sound so scholarly. Had I not experienced a different sort of church I might buy

135

their angry and impatient arguments. But *renewal is possible!* The gospel *is* relevant. Preaching, teaching, administration, and action *can* be fused into covenant response to contemporary need. Worship *can* be meaningful. And cultural involvement—social service and political action *can* grow out of our life together in the community of faith. Those who would abandon the institution just don't understand; they are dependent upon it. Even in their protest and rebellion they are sustained by it. Jerry Walker says they are like astronauts walking in space; "They are not free entities, but are tied by an umbilical cord to that larger body, the body of Christ, which sustains their ventures." [2]

However, and let me underscore this, we should not dismiss these critics of the church. In spite of what appears to be their arrogance and ingratitude they speak an essential word. We have grown defensive because we are so vulnerable—and in moments of honest candor we know it. Far too much of our institutional effort is devoted to self-preservation and denominational aggrandizement.

The church is called to a new birth; to new life in Christ. In spite of our misgivings, *this insistence upon renewal is not impertinent; it is imperative.* But where does it come from? *What are the sources of genuine church renewal?*

First (and here I sound like the old tub-thumping revivalist), *we must return to our biblical roots.* W. A. Visser 't Hooft, former general secretary of the World Council of Churches, writes, "When the Church reflects on the renewal of its own life it must . . . begin (that's where most of us are) by remembering how the life of the people of God under the Old Covenant had been renewed again and again." [3]

In the experience of the Hebrew people certain things seemed to happen.

God would act and men would acknowledge him.
Time would pass and men would forsake him.
In their rebellion men would be delivered into the hands of their enemies.
In their misery they would cry out to God.
God would hear them, and in his mercy he would *renew* their spirits.

This pattern of history was repeated over and over again in the Bible. It was the story of the Exodus. It is found in Judges, Nehemiah, and the seventy-eighth Psalm. It is the burden of the prophetic message in the Old Testament and the very heart of the New Covenant. God calls us. We turn away. In our emptiness, confusion, and fear we cry out. God hears, he responds and forgives. As Visser 't Hooft suggests, "Every true renewal of the Church is based on the hearing anew of the Word of God as it comes to us in the Bible." [4]

The Word of God must not be viewed as printers' ink on blank page, or as an out-of-date, cobweb-enmeshed library of sixty-six books. The Word of God is a *living* reality and *present* authority. It is the action and will of God spelled out in the history of a people and in the life and triumphant sacrifice of a Man. As the "Manifesto for a Renewal Movement," rightly insists, "The renewed Church must be as faithful to the biblical reality that brings it into being as to the world that calls it into service." [5]

Renewal depends upon the God who *is*. Studdert-Kennedy, writing from the trenches of France during the First World War, said it like this:

It is God alone that matters, . . . not any Church of God, or priest of God . . . or any act of God in the past . . . but it is God Himself, acting here and now upon the souls of men; it is He alone that can save the world.[6]

The British chaplain was not dismissing the importance of the Bible or the Church. He was only insisting upon the obvious. Of what value is revealed truth unless it is applied and lived? God renews through the power of his present, living Word. Wallace Fisher, who has led his dowager congregation in Lancaster, Pennsylvania, "from tradition to mission," argues that the quest for new life must begin not with current fads and practices, but with "the Scriptures' witness to the living Word." While avoiding the "deceptive trap of biblicism," he urges us to search the scriptures that we might find adequate images of servanthood.[7]

Such an encounter with the living Word will lead to an inevitable rediscovery of both "persons" and "mission."

The church has often criticized the twentieth century for dehumanizing man. Industry, it says, has put man on the assembly line and turned him into a number. Government has lost him in a welter of bureaus and agencies. Apollo flights soar toward the moon, and man, left behind, shrinks into microscopic insignificance.

But religion can lose sight of people as quickly as an insensitive culture can. That is what the parable of the Good Samaritan was all about. We have praised the hero of that story and conveniently forgotten the villains, two pious frauds who left their battered brother in the ditch while they went on about their religious duties.

The Sermon on the Mount is cluttered with timeless lessons. Among other things, it insists that codes, laws, and institutional structures exist for persons. Man was not created for the sake of traditions; traditions exist to serve man. In *Funny Girl* Barbra Streisand sang, "People who need people are the luckiest people in the world." Not only the luckiest, they are the *only* people in the world. This Jesus knew. He saw persons as ends in themselves, to be served as brothers and regarded as children of God.

Do you remember how it was with Jesus? How he took a dusty, bothersome little child into his lap and said "The kingdom of God is right here"? How he talked to a woman by a well, a woman who had been married more often than Liz Taylor, and who was living out of wedlock at that very moment; how he respected her as a *person* and discussed things that really mattered? How he sought out the sick and the put-upon and the sinful while puncturing the egos of self-satisfied religionists who thought they were too busy or too good for folk like that?

And do you remember Dives in the sixteenth chapter of Luke, how he went to hell? He was damned, not because he was malicious or brutal, but because he didn't take the time to see and care. Imagine him in today's world: breakfasting every morning in his lovely suburban home; going to work in his sleek Mark IV; whizzing right over jungles of ghetto need as he takes the expressway to the heart of the city; sprinting to his office while an attendant parks his car; slaving over graphs, charts, and sales records, pausing only for two coffee breaks and a martini lunch; then racing home again, over the foul hopelessness of the inner city, to his shower, his family, his relaxation, his world removed. The rich man died, you remember, and cried out for mercy from his place of agony; but to no avail. He would continue in torment because he had not seen or heard the human need crying out for help in his own city.

If the church is to be renewed, it must take *people* seriously, not just as membership statistics, potential givers, pins on a parish map or pew captains during institutional festivals, but as laughing, crying, dreaming, yearning, sinning people. The church must rediscover the kinds of people for whom Christ died. Only thus can it fulfill its mission, a mission that promises to take it into many a wilderness, into many a Gethsemane, and up many a cross-crowned hill.

One of the biblical definitions of the church is "the body of Christ." A body is not simply a blob of flesh. It is muscle, nerve, blood, cartilage, tissue; it is physical substance given form by skeletal structure. The body could not function without its skeleton. So too with the church. It could not be the body of Christ, extending his ministry into the here and now, unless its members were given their form and cohesion by skeletal structure. This is why the church is organized. *If the Church is to be renewed, however, it must rethink and redefine its structures in the light of person-centered mission.* As Stephen Rose has rightly said, "The institution that takes renewal seriously makes continual provision for its own transformation from one form into another." [8]

It would be nice if we could start from scratch; if some beneficent foundation would come along and provide a grant (with God's approval, of course) that would enable us to organize the ideal church. Would it have graded choirs, women's circles, men's clubs, kitchens, mimeograph machines, and massive walls in Gothic cruciform? Would it have myriad committees to care for all the busywork from tending flowers to ordering toilet paper? I don't know. I have an idea, however, that if we started with a blank sheet of paper instead of a denominational rule book we would come up with some interesting recommendations.

What if we began by returning the money to the generous foundation? (That would be our first heresy!) The early church was not endowed. Its stewardship practices would shame our own, but it seemed to have few monetary neuroses. With the money question out of the way we would be forced to put first things first. We would have to deal with the obvious. What is the true nature of this body? Who are its members? Who are its ministers? What are their ministries? Who are we here to serve? What are the unmet needs of these people? What other groups and agencies are trying to meet these needs, and how? What are the crises evident in this situation and in our world? What is being done to understand and respond to these crises? What is the distinctive contribution to be made by the Christian gospel and fellowship? How can we best make that contribution? What organizational structure will these ministries require? These are the kinds of questions our churches ought to be asking.

Most of us can't start from scratch, nor should we. We can be guided by rich traditions without being bound by them. We can draw from available resources without being subservient to them. In a word, we can utilize our present structures (in most instances they provide a tremendous "given") in preparing for better forms for mission.

I know of a huge inner-city church that has developed a commission on urban ministries. The *Discipline* of the denomination does not call for such a structure, but it permits it. Where did the commission come from? It emerged from the grass roots, from an assortment of lay-inspired and lay-directed projects. There was a community service program enrolling nearly 400 elementary school youngsters. There was a health clinic; and planned parenthood and well-baby clinics. There was a teen canteen and a thrift shop and outpost Sunday schools. The church needed to be related to the community organization in its neighborhood and to the government agencies responsible for Head Start classes that used its facilities. That particular church has abolished many of the required committees it considered excess baggage, but its mission to a radically changing, now almost totally black, neighborhood required the adding of a new one. So it was done. Just as the form of the early church grew out of the experience of the early church, so should our form, our structure, grow out of the challenge and pressure of our time.

In the final analysis, however, it will take more than the correct reading of Scripture, the rediscovery of persons and mission, and the restructuring of the institution to bring about genuine church renewal. *It will take us—and people like us.*

In the little known book of Second Chronicles we read of "Hezekiah's good reign." How did it begin? It began with the cleansing of the house of God. The doors were thrown open, the lamps were relit, the sacred fires were rekindled. A young king came to his throne believing that his nation could not be renewed until its spirit was renewed. He called together the religious people of the land, called them to genuine repentence, reminded them of their sacred ministries, and consecrated them. That is how renewal begins. With *our* penitence, confession, forgiveness, rededication; with *our own personal conse-cration.* This applies to clergy and laity alike. *We are ministers together.*

Keith Miller has spoken to hundreds of thousands of laymen through his personal testimony in *The Taste of New Wine.* An Episcopalian, he described his rebirth into a life of vital fellowship with Christ. But this new sense of commitment made him look at the church with a jaundiced eye. He knew how smug and self righteous some of its members were; how noncommittal and utterly disinterested others were. He knew how ineffective its witness was, how it spun its wheels and occupied itself with trivia. Disgusted, he drew away from it. Oh, he continued his personal devotions and family worship. He continued to meet with small groups to study and pray. He didn't surrender his faith, he just gave up on the church.

But there came a day when he realized he had been wrong. His own attitudes had helped throw up a barrier. His judgments had been immature and self-righteous. He was guilty of some of the things he freely criticized in others. He came to see that Christians have no right to cut themselves free from the church. It is the body of Christ. Its members are human, but they are called to be "different." Miller writes, "The Church cannot be the Church without a company of people with drastically changed purposes and directions, deeply motivated to be a servant people devoted to their Lord." [9] The church will be renewed as its members are renewed and as they, under God, refashion its life to meet human need. Only thus can the church's mission be fulfilled in a troubled world.

CHAPTER 13

They say that everyone has his own cross to bear, Lord. And you once said, "Take up your cross and follow me." What do these things mean? I think they mean that every person ultimately has to face up to reality—face his own destiny, his own calling, his own nature and responsibilities. . . .

The way of the cross was your understanding of your mission and your faithfulness to it.

The way of the cross seems to be, for every individual Christian, the reality which dictates his style of life, defines his own mission, and brings him into communion with you.

Help me to bear my cross on the way of the cross, Jesus.

Malcolm Boyd

THE WAY IT IS

Frank Farrar is the young governor of South Dakota. During his campaign he kept saying he was going to "tell it like it (was)." Even Richard Nixon, as he scrambled toward the presidency, told young audiences he would "tell it like it (was)." There seemed to be some special merit in the slogan. *Esquire* magazine in a recent issue suggests that certain words and phrases should be put to rest. They've been worn threadbare; we've already gotten too much mileage out of them. Some of the words were "cool," "groovy," and "bag." One of the phrases was "tell it like it is."

Why should any man pride himself on telling it like it is? To do otherwise would be to be deceitful and dishonest. Yet there are certain forms of truth that should be highlighted. One truth may be far more important than another. For instance, *the future of the church rests squarely on the shoulders of the lay ministry.* To say *that* is to tell it like it is. Elton Trueblood has written: "The number one task of our time is the enlargement and adequate training of our ministry *which . . . includes our total membership.*" [1] One essential ingredient for a new

145

church is the rebirth of the lay apostolate. There will be no renewal apart from laymen. Ecclesiastical overlords and theological pundits cannot refashion the community of faith. We are only hired hands. The church will be reborn as its rank and file discover the deepest meanings of "new life in Christ."

A few years ago I preached in South Bend, Indiana. After the service an angry listener came to me and said, "The more we pay you preachers the more you tell us *we* ought to be doing." Obviously, the church, for him, was a place to go, to sit, to listen, and to leave. Christianity was a spectator sport. An outstanding Christian leader has confessed: "Millions [of us] are merely back-seat Christians, willing to be observers of a performance the professionals put on, ready to criticize or applaud, but not willing even to consider the possibility of real participation." [2] Millions are merely back-seat Christians! That's the problem. We have missed the point, the essential genius, of the New Testament.

Christianity began as a layman's movement. The Lord of the church was neither a Sadducee nor a Pharisee; he was not a professional religionist. He was a carpenter—a *layman,* if you please. And who did he choose as his close friends and collaborators? Laymen! Layman all, with the exception of Simon the Zealot. Zealots were Pharisees with a vengeance. They were revolutionaries, who believed in a bloody overthrow of Rome. But apart from Simon, the professional troublemaker, Jesus sought out everyday kinds of people: fishermen, tax gatherers, housewives, men of the soil, a business man named Joseph, and Mary, a woman of the streets. Later there would be a physician named Luke and a tentmaker named Paul. Jesus did not recruit trained professionals. He seemed to prefer the John Does of his world; and "the common people heard him gladly."

The Roman Catholic Church has had rare insight at this point. The popes, Pius and Clement and Nicholas, have worn their ermine robes and bejewelled crowns; they have accumulated wealth and displayed power. But the *saints* of the church, canonized by Rome, have been another breed. They have largely been peasants, simple folk, the "blessed meek," who have lived close to nature and to God.

Surrounded as we are by the visible "brass" of the church—a varied assortment of ecclesiastical dignitaries—we sometimes forget that it all began at a tradesman's bench when a lowly Jew said, "The greatest among you will be the least." Lest you misunderstand, I am not anticlerical. I am not calling for a rejection of professional religious leaders. To the contrary, we need more and better clergymen today; men who are willing to pay the price, acquire the training, accept the disciplines, and run the risks required of Christian leadership. I am saying that the church must get out of its robes, out of its pulpits, beyond its cozy walls and stained-glass windows, and become a *people's movement!*

If the church is to be "new," every member must be challenged to see himself as a minister.

The late Hendrik Kraemer, a Dutch theologian and a layman, argued that no self-respecting Christian should be asked to "help" the church. That's *not* the way it is. Rather, Christians are challenged to accept "what they are by the nature and calling of Christ's Church as the 'people of God,' sent into the world for witness and service." [8] We are not here to help the Church; we *are* the Church. Arnold Come, a man greatly influenced by Kraemer, writes, "Every Christian is to regard himself as a *minister in the Church.* . . . Every member of the body of Christ must be regarded as having . . . some service to perform for the up-building of the body." [4] Do you see the implications? If your church has six hundred members it has not one minister, but six hundred. That's the way it is! At least, that's the way it should be.

I'm not downgrading ordination or selling short the priestly function of the clergy. I am only saying that Christ's ministry is far broader than order, ritual, church law, and tradition.

The ministry to which every Christian is called is not primarily church-related; it is life-related.

Where does such a ministry begin? In the most difficult place of all, the home. We wear many masks in our worlds of superficial relationships. We want employers and customers to respond to us. We want friends to like us. So we smile and pretend. But at home, among those we should love most, we let our hair down and often reveal inexcusable boorishness.

The New Testament talks about the church in the house. That is where true ministry starts because it is where most of us do most of our living. If we betray the lordship of Christ at home, then our witness will be empty elsewhere. Such a concept of ministry necessarily affects our attitudes toward sex, marriage, child-bearing, and family living.

Marriage is seen not as one of the "games people play," but as an "honorable estate instituted by God and signifying the mystical union between Christ and his Church."

Sex is viewed not as a "swinging" appendage on an

148

otherwise dull life, nor as a dirty word to be avoided, but as a sacrament; as the union of two persons in love.

The birth of a child is seen not as a nagging intrusion into our private worlds, but as a special gift and sacred trust.

The family is seen not only in its psychological and social dimensions, but also in its role as the proving ground for a life-giving faith.

It is within the family that we learn the arts of understanding, patience, loyalty, tenderness, sacrifice, forgiveness, and genuine unselfishness. The home is the basic institution of society, and if moral discipline and spiritual idealism do not come alive within the home then our ministries will have little validity outside the home.

Ministry begins at home, but it certainly doesn't stop there. In fact, many of us don't live in homes. We are alone, or we share living quarters with roommates; some of us are older and at loose ends. Where else do we do our living? *At work; on the job.* Most of our jobs are neutral. They become what we make them.

The farmer or rancher can confuse absolute self-centeredness for rugged individualism and live unto himself alone, or he can see himself as an instrument in the hand of God providing food and substance for the masses.

The merchant can enter the dog-eat-dog jungle of competition with no questions asked and no holds barred, or, through policy and practice, he can help transform the ethical climate of the community.

The politician can view an election as an end in itself and demagoguery as the means to the end, or he can view high office as public trust and launching pad for the commitments of his life.

The teacher can learn to "tolerate a bunch of brats" in order to draw a paycheck, or view the classroom as a laboratory where tomorrow's world is coming to birth and nourish her relationship to each young life committed to her care.

So it is with each of us. We can use our jobs and professions selfishly, building up our egos and bank accounts through them, or we can bring them into line with our most enlightened insights and make of them our ministries.

I once addressed a staff managers' training school for a life insurance company. I talked about the value of human life and the meaning of vocation. Following my remarks, a man came to me and said, "I've been in the insurance game for seventeen years and I've been a Baptist for as long as I can remember, but this is the first time I ever thought they had anything to do with one another." They must have! If our faith is to be exemplified in the marketplace, we must bring our five-day weeks and our Christian idealism together.

Five years ago I was in India, conducting a series of stewardship conferences with a dear missionary friend. One sunbaked day I found myself in Hyderabad, talking to S. P. Raju, an engineer and civil servant of the Indian government. He invented the smokeless *chula,* an oven intended to bring relative cleanliness to the Indian village, and designed a one-room house, approved by the government, that could revolutionize village life. Dr. Raju, in addition to being an inventor and a bureaucrat (in the best sense of that word) is also a remarkable Christian, a leader of the church of South India and a former committee chairman of the World Council of Churches. During the course of our conversation he handed me a tattered piece of paper on which he had once paraphrased words written by Paul.

Raju, a servant of Jesus Christ called to be an engineer, separated unto the Gospel of God in the evangelism of irrigation research for growing more food and bringing redemption from hunger. . . . Also separated unto the Gospel of God in the evangelism of housing research for the poor, for bringing preventive redemption to them from congestion, dirt and disease, which are the potential sources of moral evil and sin.

That is what I am talking about. His ministry has taken him into the Indian village; has guided his hand at the drawing board; has given profound meaning to a desk job and a government salary. His is a ministry as authentic as that of Pope Paul or Eugene Carson Blake.

But let's not omit the organized church from our thinking. Most of us are church members. We once vowed to support the church with our prayers, presence, gifts, and service. More important than the vow once taken, however, is *our continuing relationship to the church as the body of Christ.* As organic members of that body we are called to extend the Incarnation into this time and place.

Never has the church been more desperately needed— and I'm not simply talking about the global ministries of World Council of Churches or the cooperative projects of national church councils or the policies and pronouncements of sprawling denominational hierarchies. I am talking about your particular church, and your relationship to it, and your relationship to the larger community through it.

Let me tell you about a handful of people who have taught me more about ministry than I ever learned from textbooks or in classrooms. They are ministers of Jesus Christ, unordained, yet "called" and "sent." They *live* the gospel. They *are* the Church.

Two of them are physicians. During the Congolese crisis several years ago they volunteered to leave their practices and go to the Congo to replace other doctors who had fled. They went, entrusting their practices to professional colleagues (greater trust has no doctor than that!). For months they gave their services to a land torn by tribal warfare, that human need might be met.

One of them upon his return looked at the black neighborhood around his church. He argued that he had no right, as a Christian, to go to a distant continent to serve while ignoring the need squatting on his church's doorstep. He offered to staff a health clinic one day a week. Today, in the heart of that underprivileged neighborhood, a clinic is operated by volunteer doctors and nurses.

Another minister is an eye surgeon, who, with his wife, is concerned about the tragic subcontinent of India. Many years ago they visited hospitals and clinics there. They saw the indescribable need. Since then they have crisscrossed a three-state area appealing to churches, hospitals, and auxiliary groups for medical equipment and supplies. To date, this remarkable couple has been responsible for sending more than six tons of materials (everything from copper tubing to operating tables) valued at nearly two million dollars. Two people—the lay apostolate!

And there is the dean of girls of a fashionable suburban junior high school, who took a two-year leave of absence that she might go to Latin America, teach English in a seminary, and witness for Christ by teaching illiterate adults how to read. (While visiting her I met a ninety-year-old man she had taught to read the Bible.) She went as a volunteer.

A young college professor, with his wife, was concerned about underprivileged children who lived near their church. He challenged a group of students in his school to help in a community service program. Today there are scores of such volunteers, college and seminary students and members of that church, helping schoolchildren with their reading and math, teaching them how to cook and sew, relating the love of Christ to his world.

And there was Wenonah Hatfield, my secretary and the most Christlike person I have ever known. Her father was killed in an automobile accident many years ago, and following his death she lovingly cared for an invalid mother. Their life together was beautiful. They lived in a black neighborhood, and every Thursday night their home was open to neighbors for a community prayer meeting. There was nothing stilted or formal about Wenonah's prayer life. The Christ of God was an indwelling Spirit and constant companion. She did what she did because of the inspiration of his presence. She gathered clothing for the children of a prostitute who lived next door. She befriended an assortment of strange and needy people. Often her phone rang through the night as they called, seeking a listening ear and prayerful counsel.

Nine years ago Wenonah saw four little Negro youngsters playing in front of her house. She invited them in, fed them cookies and Kool-Aid, and told them Bible stories. That was the beginning of an Outpost Sunday school. For seven years Wenonah met with these youngsters, more than fifty of them, every Sunday afternoon. She took them to the zoo, to ball games, to restaurants. They were her very special "family."

Six years ago one of her girls, six-year-old Stephanie, was dying of leukemia. At Wenonah's request I visited little Stephanie in the hospital. Stephanie's father was there, a ne'er-do-well who had been released from the county jail to see his critically ill daughter. Her mother, a strong and noble woman who worked as a maid and housekeeper, and Wenonah were there, too. We went into the white, antiseptic hospital room. We talked. Time came to leave. I asked if Stephanie wanted prayer. She nodded and reached her little black hand out for Wenonah; and Wenonah, who was her very special minister, prayed. Never have I sensed the presence of God more vividly. Stephanie died. The funeral home prepared a little two-page bulletin. One page carried the order of worship for the funeral. The other page carried an all-too-brief biography. Among other things, however, the short sketch said that Stephanie was a charter member of Broadway's Sunday school. Not quite, for that would have taken her back to 1873. But she was proud of her relationship to that church, as the church had every right to be proud of its relationship to her—and all because of Wenonah.

Shortly after we left Indianapolis, Wenonah died. After suffering for more than two years, she quietly succumbed to cancer. Her mother was there, in her wheelchair, by her side. The neighbors—all Negroes, remember—wrote a letter to Mrs. Hatfield and the family. I read it as a part of her memorial service.

We the neighbors of Winthrop Avenue, wish to express our deepest and heartfelt sympathy. We would like for you to know that we too have lost a friend; a friend indeed. A friend that comes along once in a lifetime. But our loss is sure heaven's gain. We are proud to have known her for her Christian work and her saintly way of living. We saw her daily and not one time did we see her without that smile, that only a child of God could wear. She was the founder of the Children's Sunday School in our neighborhood; that started in her home and grew so rapidly that more teachers and homes had to be used. Never was it too cold nor too hot to see her going about the neighborhood winning children's hearts to Jesus. Dear ones in Christ we could go on and on telling of the good things she stood for. But in closing may we say: Sleep, sleep our loved one and we will try to carry on as you wish.

There you have it. That is the meaning and the consequence of Christian ministry. Through our homes, in our work lives, and through our faithful churchmanship, we will make Christ come alive in the commonplace events of everyday. Only thus can the church be renewed. It depends upon us—upon each of us—and upon our response to the One who said, "If any man will come after me let him deny himself, take up his cross daily and follow me."

This is the way it is—the way of the cross—there's no other way but this.

155

NOTES

INTRODUCTION

1. Robert Graham Kemper, "Ministry Begins at 40," *The Pulpit* XL (September 1969), 3.
2. Robert G. Middleton, "From Launching Pad to Orbit," *The Pulpit* XL (July-August 1969), 3.
3. Stephen C. Rose, *The Grass Roots Church* (Apex Book; Nashville: Abingdon Press, 1968). See chapter 7.
4. James A. Pike, *A New Look in Preaching* (New York: Charles Scribner's Sons, 1961), p. 31.

CHAPTER 1

1. Louis Cassels, *The Real Jesus* (New York: Doubleday & Co., 1968).
2. Anonymous, "Africa," *The Story of Jesus in the World's Literature*, ed. Edward Wagenknecht (New York: Creative Age Press, 1946), p. 254.
3. Budd Schulberg, *Waterfront* (New York: Random House, 1955), pp. 225-26.

CHAPTER 2

1. Bob Dylan, "Blowing in the Wind."
2. *Ibid.*
3. Dietrich Bonhoeffer, ed. Eberhard Bethge, *Ethics* (Macmillan Paperback; The Macmillan Co., 1965), p. 194.
4. H. C. N. Williams, "Some Starting Points for Christian Renewal," *Church in Metropolis*, p. 7.

CHAPTER 3

1. Colin Morris, *Include Me Out* (Nashville: Abingdon Press, 1968), p. 7.
2. *Ibid.*, p. 70.
3. Doug LeMaster, "Little Tree."

157

4. Morris, *Include Me Out,* p. 68.
5. William P. Merrill, "Rise Up, O Men of God." Used by permission of *The Presbyterian Outlook,* Richmond, Virginia.

CHAPTER 4
1. William Sloan Coffin, "Playboy Interview," *Playboy,* August 1968, p. 138.
2. Michael Harrington, *The Accidental Century* (New York: The Macmillan Co., 1965), p. 145.

CHAPTER 5
1. John H. Griffin, *Black Like Me (Boston:* Houghton-Mifflin, 1961), p. iii.
2. Quoted in *Cavalier,* October 1969, p. 71.
3. *The Christian Century,* August 6, 1969, p. 1042.
4. *Ebony,* March 1968, p. 176.
5. James Cone, *Black Theology and Black Power* (New York: Seabury Press, 1969), p. 31.

CHAPTER 6
1. Paxton Hibben, *Henry Ward Beecher: An American Portrait* (New York: The Readers Club, 1942), p. xiv.
2. *Ibid.,* p. vii.
3. Kerner Report, p. 305.
4. *Time,* September 12, 1969, p. 17.

CHAPTER 7
1. John D. Rockefeller III, "In Praise of Young Revolutionaries," *Saturday Review,* December 14, 1968, p. 19.
2. Milton Mayer, "The Children's Crusade," *The Center Magazine,* September 1969, pp. 6, 7.
3. *Ibid.,* p. 2.
4. Rockefeller, "Young Revolutionaries," p. 19.

CHAPTER 9

1. Sid Moody, *The Denver Post,* July 13, 1969, p. 32.
2. *Life,* July 4, 1969, p. 60*b.*
3. *Christianity Today,* July 18, 1969, p. 6.
4. Lindbergh, *Letter,* p. 60*b.*
5. Cale Young Rice, "The Mystic," *The Best Poetic Work of Cale Young Rice,* ed. Laban Lacy Rice (Lebanon, Tenn.: Cumberland University Press, 1943).
6. Edward M. Hutchings, Jr., ed., *Frontiers in Science* (New York: Basic Books, 1958), p. 316.

CHAPTER 11

1. T. R. Glover, *The Jesus of History* (New York: Harper, 1950).
2. Albert C. Outler, ed., *John Wesley* (New York: Oxford University Press, 1964), p. viii.
3. *Minneapolis Tribune,* September 9, 1969, p. 13.
4. See Lee C. Moorehead, *The Freedom of the Pulpit* (Nashville: Abingdon Press 1961) p. 51.

CHAPTER 12

1. Southcott, *The Parish Comes Alive* (New York: Morehouse-Barlow, 1956), p. 60.
2. Jerry Walker, "Let Renewal Begin from Within," *Christian Advocate,* September 8, 1966, p. 8.
3. William A. Visser 't Hooft, *The Renewal of the Church* (Philadelphia: Westminster Press, 1957), p. 15.
4. *Ibid.,* p. 91.
5. *Renewal,* February 1966.
6. *The Hardest Part,* p. 1.
7. Wallace E. Fisher, *From Tradition to Mission* (Nashville: Abingdon Press, 1965). See chapter 2.
8. Rose, *The Grass Roots Church,* p. 17.

9. Keith Miller, *A Second Touch* (Waco, Tex.: Word Books, 1967), p. 115.

CHAPTER 13

1. Elton Trueblood, *The Company of the Committed* (New York: Harper & Row, 1961), p. 57.
2. *Ibid.*
3. Hendrik Kraemer, *A Theology of the Laity* (Philadelphia: Westminster Press, 1959), p. 167.
4. Arnold B. Come, *Agents of Reconciliation* (Philadelphia: Westminster Press, 1964), p. 103.